Using the Standards
Geometry

Grade 3

Published by Instructional Fair
an imprint of
Frank Schaffer Publications®

Instructional Fair

Development House: MATHQueue, Inc.

Frank Schaffer Publications®

Instructional Fair is an imprint of Frank Schaffer Publications.

Printed in the United States of America. All rights reserved. Limited Reproduction Permission: Permission to duplicate these materials is limited to the person for whom they are purchased. Reproduction for an entire school or school district is unlawful and strictly prohibited. Frank Schaffer Publications is an imprint of School Specialty Children's Publishing. Copyright © 2005 School Specialty Children's Publishing.

Send all inquiries to:
Frank Schaffer Publications
3195 Wilson Drive NW
Grand Rapids, Michigan 49544

Using the Standards: Geometry—Grade 3

ISBN: 0-7424-2983-0

1 2 3 4 5 6 7 8 9 10 MAL 10 09 08 07 06 05

Table of Contents

Introduction 4–5
Standards Correlation Chart . . 6
Pretest 7–8

Relationships
Intersecting and Parallel Lines . . 9
The Size of Angles 10
Which Angle Is Which? 11
What Did the Right
   Angle Say? 12–13
Parallel and Perpendicular
   Lines 14
The Angles of Time. 15
All Circle Round the Polygons . 16
Shape to Shape 17
Plane Figures 18
Sides and Vertices 19
More About Sides and
   Vertices 20
Quadrilateral Names 21
Divide and Conquer 22
Drawing Triangles Based
   on Sides 23
Drawing Triangles Based
   on Angles 24
A Race to the Finish 25
Which Shape Was Drawn? . . . 26
How Many Faces and Edges? . 27
Plane and Solid Figures 28
Solid Figures 29
Can You Find the Hidden
   Shapes? 30–31
What Solid Figure Am I? 32
Exploring Solid Figures 33
Be a Builder 34
Creating Similar Polygons . . . 35
Symmetry in Letters 36
Crossword Shapes 37–38
Create Your Own Problems . . 39
Check Your Skills 40–41

Locations
Going Places 42
Following the Course 43
Reveal the Hidden
   Message 44–45
Polygon Point Plotting 46
Name the Vertices 47
Where Is Mr. Smith Going? . . 48
One Point Makes All the
   Difference 49
Crazy for Coasters 50
More About Graphing Points . 51
How Far From Point to Point? . 52
Locate the Endpoints 53
From Here to There 54
Who Gets There First? 55
Making a Course 56
Carving a Jack-o-Lantern 57
Drawing Lines of Symmetry . . 58
Create with Symmetry 59
Reflect Each Other 60
Look in the Mirror 61
Create Your Own Problems . . 62
Check Your Skills 63–64

Transformations
Flips, Slides, and Turns 65
Match the Transformation . . . 66
Are You Seeing Double? 67
Slide from Start to Finish 68
Transforming Letters 69
Transforming a Clown 70
Letter Look Alikes 71
Create Congruent Figures . . . 72
Moving to the Next Location . 73
Lines of Symmetry 74
Many Lines of Symmetry 75
Point Symmetry 76
Pictures with Point Symmetry . 77
Arrange Flowers 78
Create Your Own Problems . . 79
Check Your Skills 80–81

Modeling
Shape Scavenger Hunt 82
Patterns of Shapes 83
Use Dot Paper to Draw 84
Isosceles Drawings 85
Triangle Types 86
Draw Quadrilaterals 87
Solid Figure Scavenger Hunt . . 88
Rectangular Prism Dot-to-Dot . 89
Square Pyramid Dot-to-Dot . . 90
Face by Face 91
The Face That Does Not
   Belong 92
Patterns of Solid Figures 93
Making a Cube 94
Making a Pyramid 95
Draw the Nets 96
Drawing Shapes 97
What Will I Make? 98
Perimeters on Dot Paper 99
Playground Perimeter 100
Areas on Dot Paper 101
Dollhouse Area 102
Perimeter or Area 103
A Different View 104
Build from a View 105
Create Your Own Problems . . 106
Check Your Skills 107–108

Post Test 109–110
Answer Key 111–120
Vocabulary Cards 121–128

Introduction

This book is designed around the standards from the National Council of Teachers of Mathematics (NCTM), with a focus on geometry. Students will build new mathematical knowledge, solve problems in context, apply and adapt appropriate strategies, and reflect on processes.

The NCTM process standards are also incorporated throughout the activities. The correlation chart on page 6 identifies the pages on which each NCTM geometry substandard appears. Also look for the following process icons on each page.

 Problem Solving   Communication   Reasoning and Proof

 Connections   Representation

Workbook Pages: These activities can be done independently, in pairs, or in groups. The problems are designed to stimulate higher-level thinking skills and address a variety of learning styles.

Problems may be broken into parts with class discussion following student work. At times solution methods or representations are suggested in the activities. Students may gravitate toward using these strategies, but they should also be encouraged to create and share their own strategies.

Many activities will lead into subjects that could be investigated or discussed further as a class. You may want to compare different solution methods or discuss how to select a valid solution method for a particular problem.

Communication: Most activities have a communication section. These questions may be used as journal prompts, writing activities, or discussion prompts. Each communication question is labeled **THINK** or **DO MORE**.

Introduction (cont.)

Create Your Own Problems: These pages prompt students to create problems like those they completed on the workbook pages. Encourage students to be creative and to use their everyday experiences. The students' responses will help you to assess their practical knowledge of the topic.

Check Your Skills: These activities provide a representative sample of the types of problems developed throughout each section. These can be used as additional practice or as assessment tools.

Vocabulary Cards: Use the vocabulary cards to familiarize students with mathematical language. The pages may be copied, cut, and pasted onto index cards. Paste the front and back on the same index card to make flash cards, or paste each side on separate cards to use in matching games or activities.

Assessment: Assessment is an integral part of the learning process and can include observations, conversations, interviews, interactive journals, writing prompts, and independent quizzes or tests. Classroom discussions help students learn the difference between poor, good, and excellent responses. Scoring guides can help analyze students' responses. The following is a possible list of problem-solving steps. Modify this list as necessary to fit specific problems.

1—Student understands the problem and knows what he or she is being asked to find.

2—Student selects an appropriate strategy or process to solve the problem.

3—Student is able to model the problem with appropriate manipulatives, graphs, tables, pictures, or computations.

4—Student is able to clearly explain or demonstrate his or her thinking and reasoning.

NCTM Standards Correlation Chart

		Problem Solving	Reasoning and Proof	Communication	Connections	Representation
Relationships	identify and analyze 2-D and 3-D shapes	22, 24, 33,	9, 11, 12, 13,	9, 10, 12,	14, 17, 20,	10, 11, 14, 15,
	classify shapes					
	subdivide and combine 2-D and 3-D shapes	34, 36,	16, 18, 19, 20,	13, 15, 16,	28, 29, 30,	17, 18, 22, 23,
	explore congruence and similarity	37, 38	21, 26, 27, 33,	21, 31, 34	31, 35	24, 25, 26, 27, 28,
	make and test conjectures		35, 36			29, 32, 37, 38
Locations	describe location and movement	43, 44, 45	52, 53, 59	42, 43, 48, 50, 54	42, 50,	44, 45, 46, 47,
	use coordinate grids					
	find horizontal and vertical distance	46, 54, 55		56, 57, 58, 59	60, 61	49, 51, 57, 58
Transformations	predict and describe flips, slides, and turns	67, 68, 71	67, 68, 71	66, 76, 77	77, 78	65, 66, 69,
	show congruence using motion		73, 74, 75			
	identify line and rotational symmetry					70, 72, 74, 75
Modeling	build and draw geometric objects	91, 98, 100,	83, 92, 93	86, 87,	82, 88, 96,	82, 84, 85, 86,
	identify 2-D representations of 3-D objects	102, 103		92, 97	100, 102, 103	87, 88, 89, 90, 91,
	use models to solve problems in number and measurement					94, 95, 96, 97, 98,
	apply geometry in everyday life					99, 101, 104, 105

The pretest, post test, Create Your Own Problems, and Check Your Skills pages are not included on this chart, but contain a representative sampling of the process standards. Many pages also contain THINK or DO MORE sections, which encourage students to communicate about what they have learned.

Name _____ Date _____

Pretest

1. Circle the lines that are parallel.

2. Is the shape below a polygon? Write yes or no.

   _____

3. Which solid figure has 6 faces of equal size?

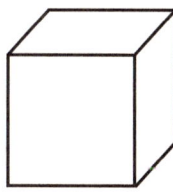   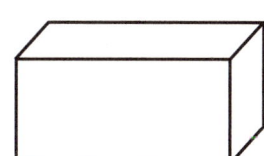   _____

Figure A   Figure B

4. Name the ordered pair for each vertex of the triangle.

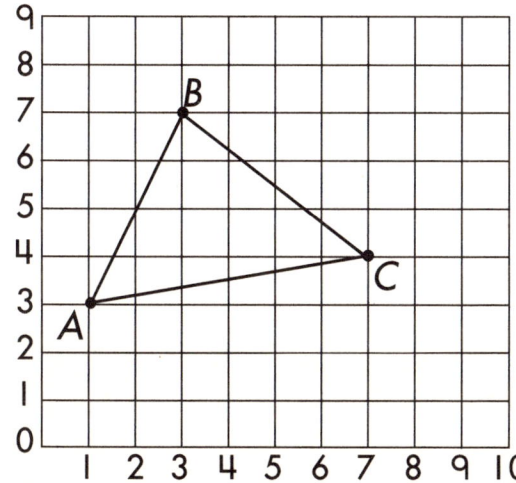

A _____

B _____

C _____

Pretest (cont.)

5. How many lines of symmetry does the plane figure have?

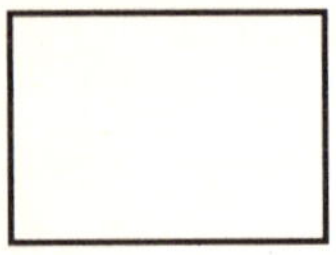

   _____

6. What is the distance (in units) of line segment AB?

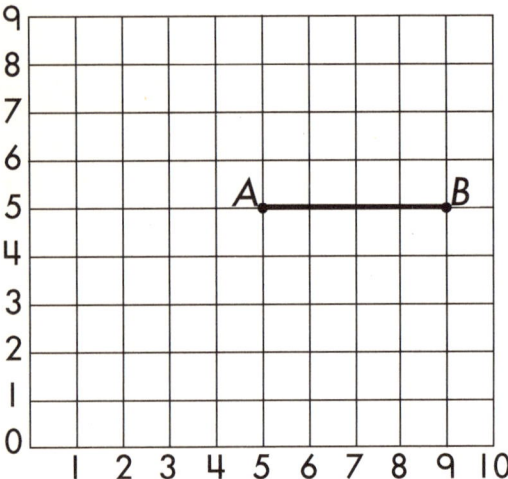   _____

7. Which transformation was performed? Circle the correct answer.

    slide

flip

turn

8. Draw the plane figure that is next in the pattern.

      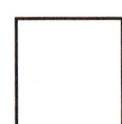 _____

Relationships  Name _____ Date _____

Intersecting and Parallel Lines

Lines that cross each other at one point are **intersecting lines**.

Lines that do not intersect each other are **parallel lines**. ⟷ ⟷

Directions: Name each set of lines as parallel or intersecting.

1.

   _____

2. ⟷
   ⟷

   _____

3.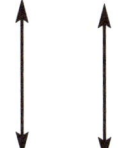

   _____

4.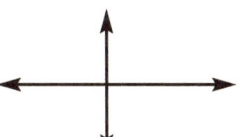

   _____

5.

   _____

THINK

 Explain how you decided which sets of lines were parallel.

Relationships

Name _____ Date _____

The Size of Angles

Two rays with a common endpoint form an **angle**.
An angle that forms a square corner is a **right angle**.

Directions: Describe each angle as a right angle, less than a right angle, or greater than a right angle.

1.   _____

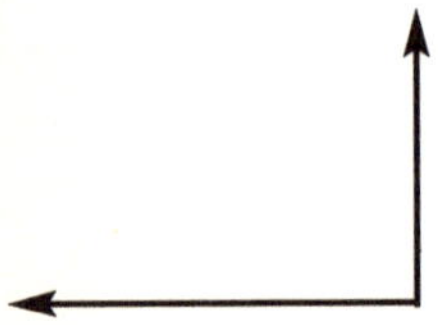

2.   _____

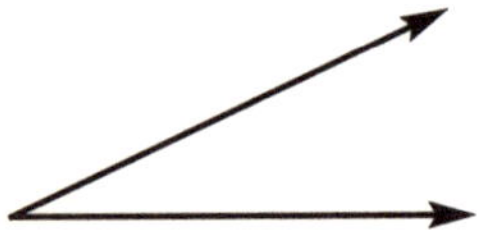

3.   _____

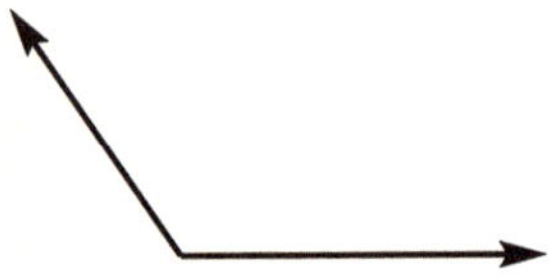

4.   _____

5.   _____

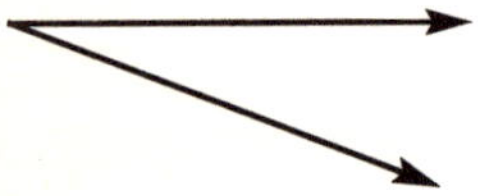

Relationships

Name _____ Date _____

Which Angle Is Which?

An angle whose measure is smaller than a right angle is an **acute angle**.
An angle whose measure is larger than a right angle is an **obtuse angle**.

Directions: Circle the acute angles.
Put a box around the obtuse angles.

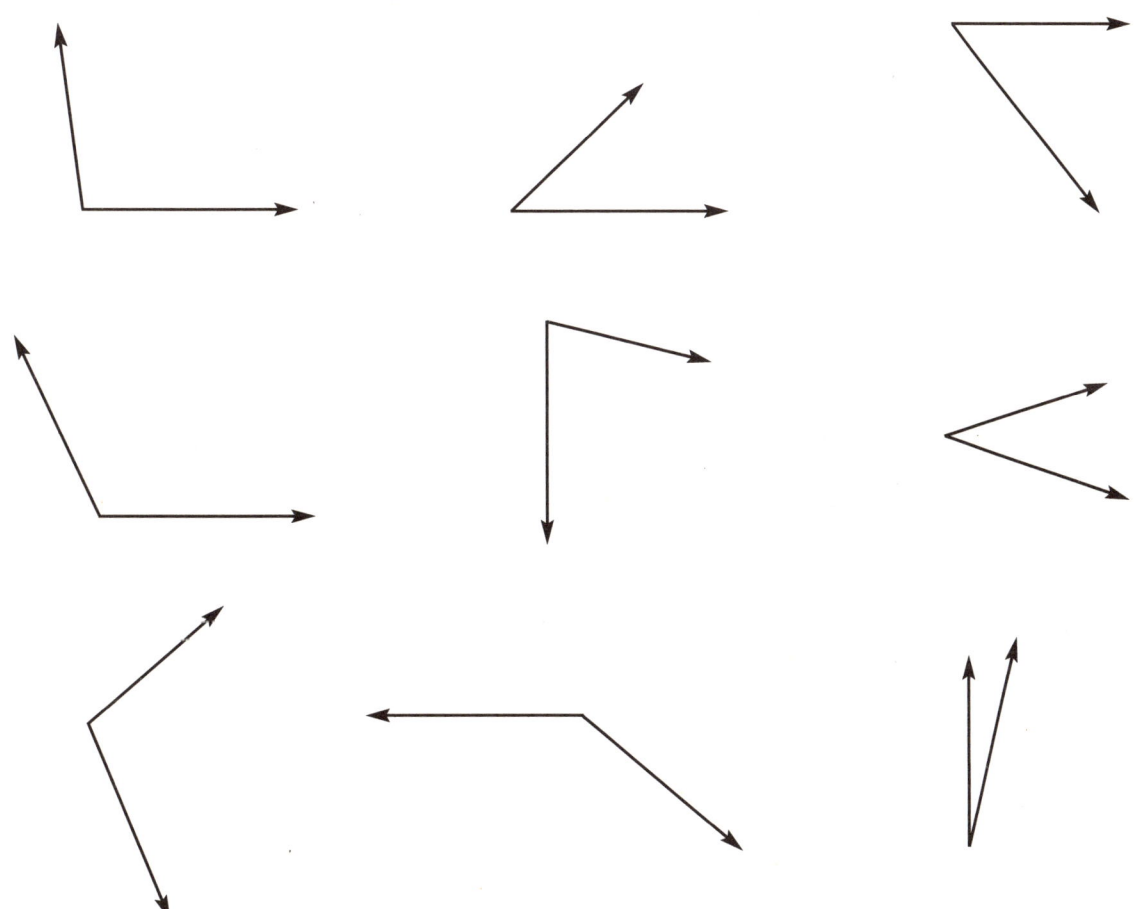

THINK

Choose an angle you circled, and explain why you circled it.
Choose an angle you put a box around, and explain why you boxed it.

Relationships   Name _____ Date _____

What Did the Right Angle Say?

Riddle: What did the right angle say to the acute angle?

Directions: To solve the riddle on page 13, first answer the following questions. Circle the letter of the correct answer.

1. Which set of lines is parallel?

   A    **B**

2. Which set of figures is congruent?

   M 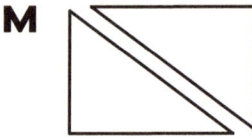   **N**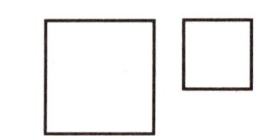

3. Which is an obtuse angle?

   S 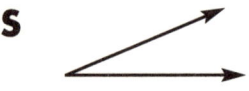   **U**

4. Does the letter **R** have a line of symmetry?

   D yes   **E** no

5. Which shape is the face of a cone?

   S

Relationships

Name _____ Date _____

What Did the Right Angle Say?

Directions: Write the letter of your answers from page 12 in the blanks below. Some blanks have already been filled for you.

    For blanks marked 1, write the letter of your answer to question 1.
    For blanks marked 2, write the letter of your answer to question 2.
    For blanks marked 3, write the letter of your answer to question 3.
    For blanks marked 4, write the letter of your answer to question 4.
    For blanks marked 5, write the letter of your answer to question 5.

<u>l</u>   <u> </u> <u> </u>   <u> </u> <u>s</u> <u> </u> <u>d</u>
 1   1 2   3   4

<u> </u> <u>o</u>   <u> </u> <u> </u> <u>k</u> <u> </u>   <u> </u>
 5   2 1   4   1

<u>s</u> <u>q</u> <u> </u> <u> </u> <u>r</u> <u> </u>.
     3 1   4

Nice Work!

Relationships     Name _____   Date _____

Parallel and Perpendicular Lines

Lines that intersect each other to form right angles are **perpendicular lines**.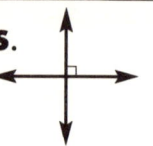

Lines that do not intersect each other are **parallel lines**.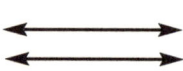

Directions: Tell whether each set of lines is parallel, perpendicular, or neither. Circle the correct answer choice.

1.  parallel perpendicular neither

2.  parallel perpendicular neither

3.  parallel perpendicular neither

4.  parallel perpendicular neither

5. 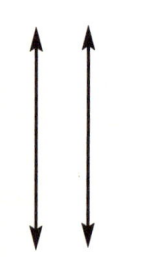 parallel perpendicular neither

6. 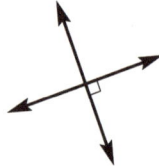 parallel perpendicular neither

THINK

 Look around the room. Do the sides of a door model parallel or perpendicular lines? Does the corner of this piece of paper model parallel or perpendicular lines?

Relationships

Name _____ Date _____

The Angles of Time

Directions: Tell whether the hands on each clock form a right angle, an acute angle, or an obtuse angle.

1.  _____

2.  _____

3.  _____

4.  _____

5.  _____

6.  _____

THINK

Name two times when the hands of the clock do not form an acute angle, obtuse angle, or right angle.

Relationships

Name _____ Date _____

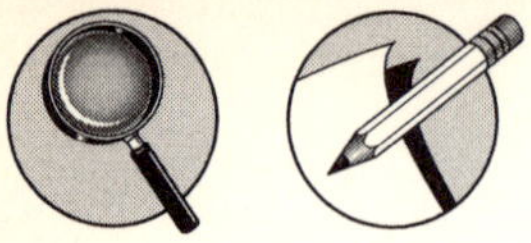

All Circle Round the Polygons

A **polygon** is closed plane figure that is formed by three or more line segments.

Directions: Circle the polygons.

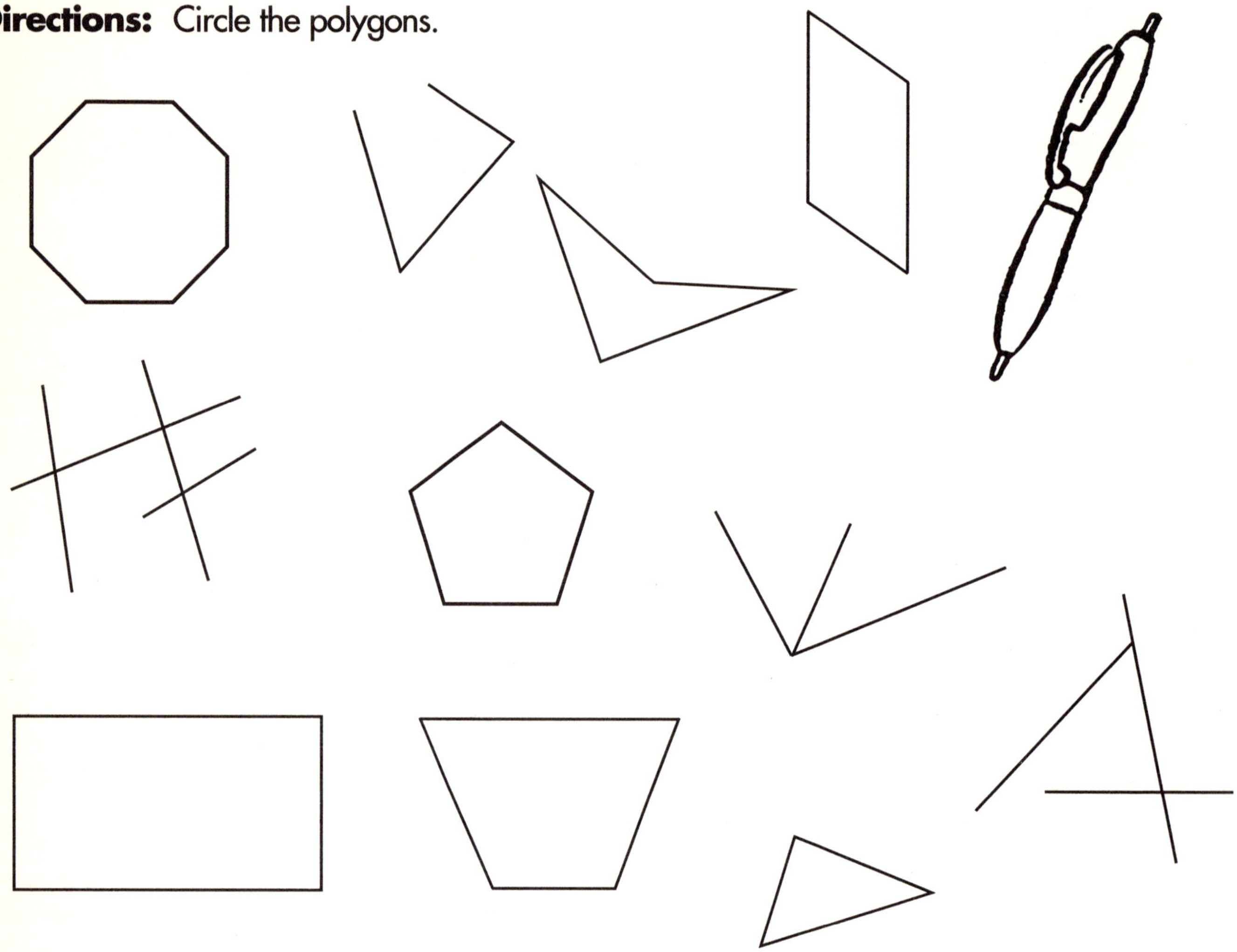

THINK

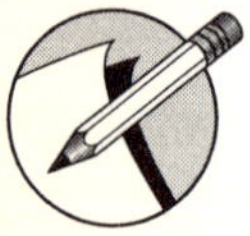

Choose one figure you circled above, and tell why you circled it.

Choose one figure you did not circle above, and tell why you did not circle it.

Relationships

Shape to Shape

Plane figures have two dimensions.
Examples of plane figures are:

| rectangle | circle | triangle | parallelogram |
| trapezoid | square | hexagon | octagon |

Directions: Name each shape shown.

1.
   _____

2.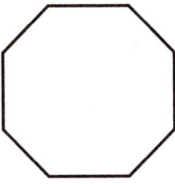
   _____

3.
   _____

4.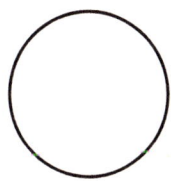
   _____

DO MORE

In the space below, draw each shape named in the box above that was not included in 1–4.

Relationships   Name _____ Date _____

Plane Figures

The following are some plane figures.

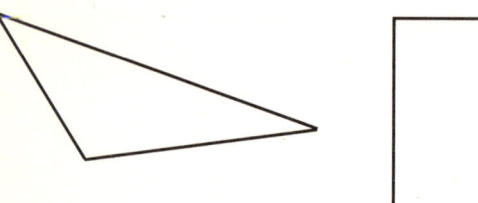 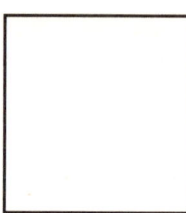 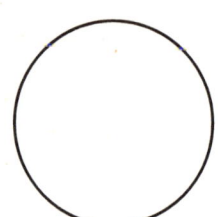 

Directions: Match each figure below with its name.
List the letters in the blanks.

1. circle _____

2. triangle _____

3. square _____

4. rectangle _____

 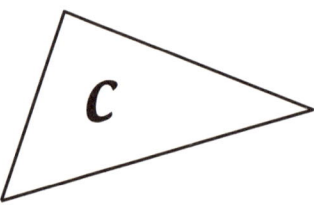 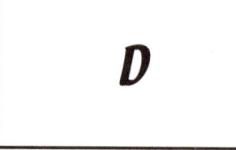

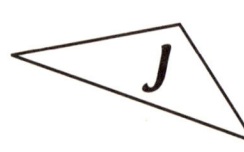  

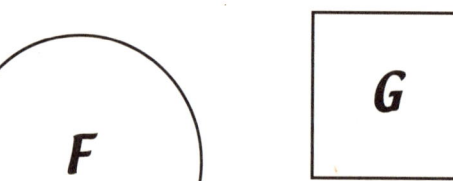

Relationships   Name _____   Date _____

Sides and Vertices

Each **side** of a polygon is a line segment.
The point where two sides meet is a **vertex**.

vertex ─○   ─ side

Vertices is the plural form of vertex.

Directions: Fill in the blanks.

1.    number of sides _____ number of vertices _____

2.    number of sides _____ number of vertices _____

3.    number of sides _____ number of vertices _____

4. 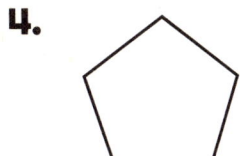   number of sides _____ number of vertices _____

5. 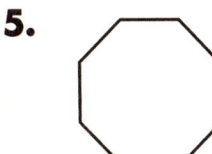   number of sides _____ number of vertices _____

Relationships   Name _____ Date _____

More About Sides and Vertices

Directions: Fill in the blanks.

1. Look at the figures on page 19. What do you notice about the number of sides and the number of vertices in each plane figure?
   _____

2. A figure with 7 sides has _____ vertices.

3. A figure with 9 sides has _____ vertices.

4. A figure with 8 sides has _____ vertices.

Directions: Answer the following questions.
Draw a picture of each of your answers.

5. Which plane figure has 5 sides and 5 vertices?

6. Which plane figure has 6 sides and 6 vertices?

DO MORE

Draw a figure with 7 sides and 7 vertices.
Draw a figure with 8 sides and 8 vertices.
Draw a figure with 9 sides and 9 vertices.

Relationships Name _____ Date _____

Quadrilateral Names

Directions: Draw a line from each shape to its name.
You may draw more than one line from each shape.
Keep this in mind: Every square is also a rectangle, but not every rectangle is a square!

1.  quadrilateral

2.  parallelogram

3.  rectangle

4. 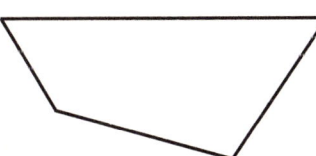 square

5.  trapezoid

DO MORE

 List four other names you can give a square.

Relationships Name _____ Date _____

Divide and Conquer

Directions: Draw line segments to divide each figure into the shapes named.

1.  [rectangle]   make 2 triangles

2. 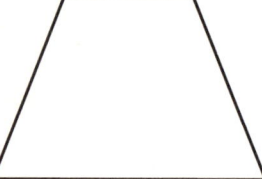   make 2 triangles and 1 rectangle

3. 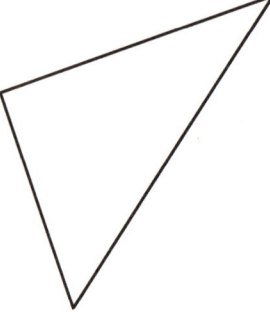   make 2 triangles

4.    make 2 squares

DO MORE

 Draw a parallelogram. Draw line segments to divide it into other shapes. Name the shapes.

Drawing Triangles Based on Sides

An **equilateral triangle** has 3 sides of equal length.

An **isosceles triangle** has 2 sides of equal length.

A **scalene triangle** has no sides of equal length.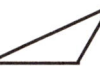

Directions: Draw the triangle described using the line segment given. You need a ruler.

1. Draw a scalene triangle using this segment as one of its sides.

2. Draw an equilateral triangle using this segment as one of its sides.

3. Draw an isosceles triangle using this segment as one of its sides.

Relationships

Name _____ Date _____

Drawing Triangles Based on Angles

Directions: Draw each triangle described.

1. an isosceles triangle with 3 acute angles

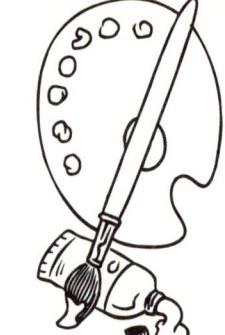

2. an isosceles triangle with 1 obtuse angle

3. an isosceles triangle with 1 right angle

4. an equilateral triangle

5. a scalene triangle with 1 right angle

6. a scalene triangle with 1 obtuse angle

THINK

How many obtuse angles can be in a triangle?
How many right angles can be in a triangle?

Relationships

Name _____ Date _____

A Race to the Finish

Directions: Play this game with a friend. You need game pieces and a coin. You can use counters. Flip a coin.

If the coin lands heads up, move forward 1 space.
If the coin lands tails up, move forward 2 spaces.

When you land on a rectangle move forward 3 spaces.
When you land on a right triangle move 2 spaces back.
When you land on a trapezoid move forward 4 spaces.

The first one to FINISH wins.

You are a winner!

Relationships     Name _____   Date _____

Which Shape Was Drawn?

Directions: Which figure did each person draw? Circle the figure.

1. Jackson drew a figure that had 2 pairs of parallel sides.

   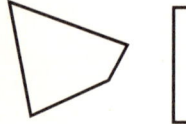   

2. Angie drew a figure that had 4 right angles.

3. Joel drew a figure that had only 1 pair of parallel sides.

    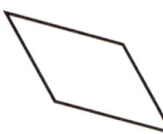 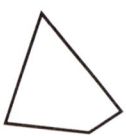 

4. Nadia drew a figure that had 4 sides of equal length.

5. Belle drew a figure that did not have any parallel sides.

     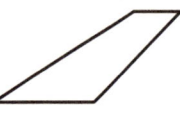 

DO MORE

 Write a problem like the ones above to share with a friend.

Relationships Name _____ Date _____

How Many Faces and Edges?

A **face** is a flat surface of a solid figure.
The place where two faces of a solid figure meet is an **edge**.

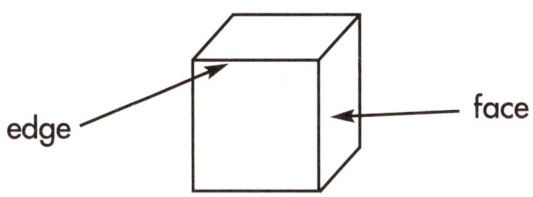

Directions: Fill in the blanks.

1. 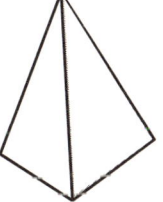   number of faces _____ number of edges _____

2. 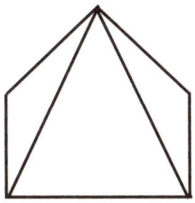   number of faces _____ number of edges _____

3. 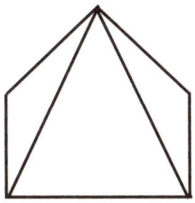   number of faces _____ number of edges _____

4. 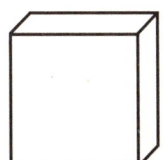   number of faces _____ number of edges _____

Relationships Name _____ Date _____

Plane and Solid Figures

Directions: Identify each object as a plane figure or a solid figure. Circle the correct answer choice.

1. 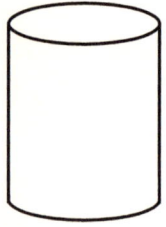   plane figure   solid figure

2. 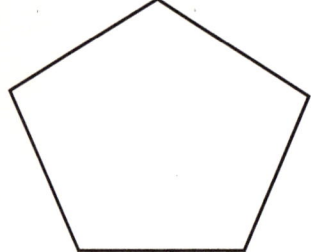   plane figure   solid figure

3. 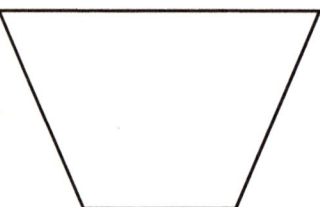   plane figure   solid figure

4. 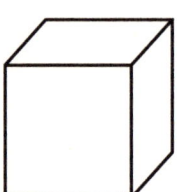   plane figure   solid figure

Relationships

Name _____ Date _____

Solid Figures

Directions: Name the solid figure that each object models.

1.

   _____

2.

   _____

3.

   _____

4.

   _____

5.

   _____

6.

   _____

Relationships  Name _____ Date _____

Can You Find the Hidden Shapes?

Directions: Carefully look at each picture below. Then turn to page 31 and answer the questions.

A

B

C

D

E

F

G

Relationships

Name _____ Date _____

Can You Find the Hidden Shapes?

Directions: Answer each question. Name each picture on page 30 by its letter. Name the objects that model the solid figures.

1. Where are the spheres?

   _____
   _____
   _____

2. Where are the cones?

   _____
   _____
   _____

3. Where are the cylinders?

   _____
   _____
   _____

4. Where are the rectangular solids?

   _____
   _____
   _____

Relationships

Name _____ Date _____

What Solid Figure Am I?

Directions: Determine the solid figure from each set of clues. Draw a picture of each solid figure.

1. I have six faces. All of my edges are equal in length.

2. I only have one flat face. My face is a circle.

3. I have 5 faces. One of my faces is a square. My other faces are triangles.

4. I have no flat faces and no edges, but I am a solid figure.

5. I have the same number of faces as a cube. My edges are not equal in length.

DO MORE

Describe a solid that is different from the ones above.

Relationships

Name _____ Date _____

Exploring Solid Figures

Directions: Answer each question.

1. If you want to stack two of these solid figures, which would have to be on the bottom? _____

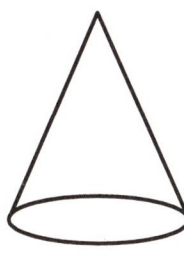

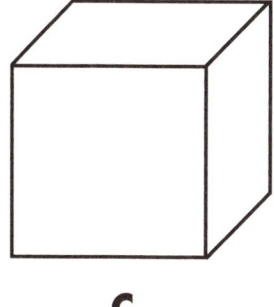

A   B   C

2. If you want to stack all of these solid figures, which would have to be on the top? _____

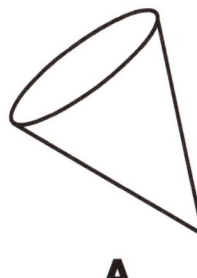

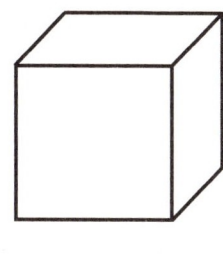

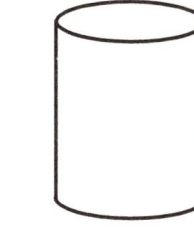

A   B   C

Relationships

Name _____ Date _____

Be a Builder

Directions: Combine at least two of the shapes below to create each figure named. You can turn the shapes.

You can use more than one of the same shape.

You can even change the size of the shape.

 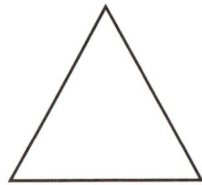  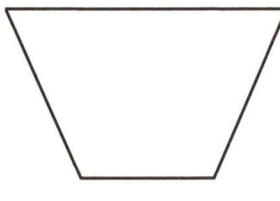

1. house

2. teepee

3. castle

4. sailboat

THINK

Describe how you built the house using these shapes.

Is there another way to build a house using these shapes? Explain.

Relationships

Name _____ Date _____

Creating Similar Polygons

Similar figures have the same shape.
Similar figures do not have to be, but can be the same size.
Their sides do have to be proportional in size.

Corresponding sides of similar polygons have lengths that are proportional.
Corresponding angles of similar polygons have equal measures.

Directions: Use a ruler to draw similar figures. Draw the second polygon using the information given.

1. Draw a rectangle similar to the one shown. The rectangle given should be two times bigger than the one you draw.

   [rectangle: 2 inches by 1 inch]

2. Draw a right triangle similar to the one shown. The triangle you draw should be four times the size than the one shown.

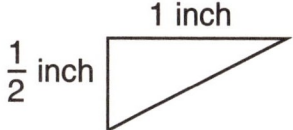

THINK

Explain how you found the length of each side of the polygons you drew.

Relationships

Name _____ Date _____

Symmetry in Letters

Directions: Draw lines of symmetry in each of the letters below.

THINK

 Which letters have more than one line of symmetry?

Relationships Name _____ Date _____

Crossword Shapes

Directions: Answer each question. Place the word in the proper spaces in the crossword puzzle on page 38.

Across

2. The shape of a basketball.
3. A plane figure with no vertices.
5. The plane figure with 3 sides.
7. The solid figure with 6 faces of equal size.
9. The shape of a soup can.
10. The face of a cube.

Down

1. A place where line segments meet in a plane figure.
4. The plane figure with the four right angles and same number of edges as a square.
6. Where two faces of a solid figure meet.
8. The solid figure that has all triangles for its faces.

Relationships

Name _____ Date _____

Crossword Shapes

Directions: Place your answers from page 37 in the crossword puzzle below.

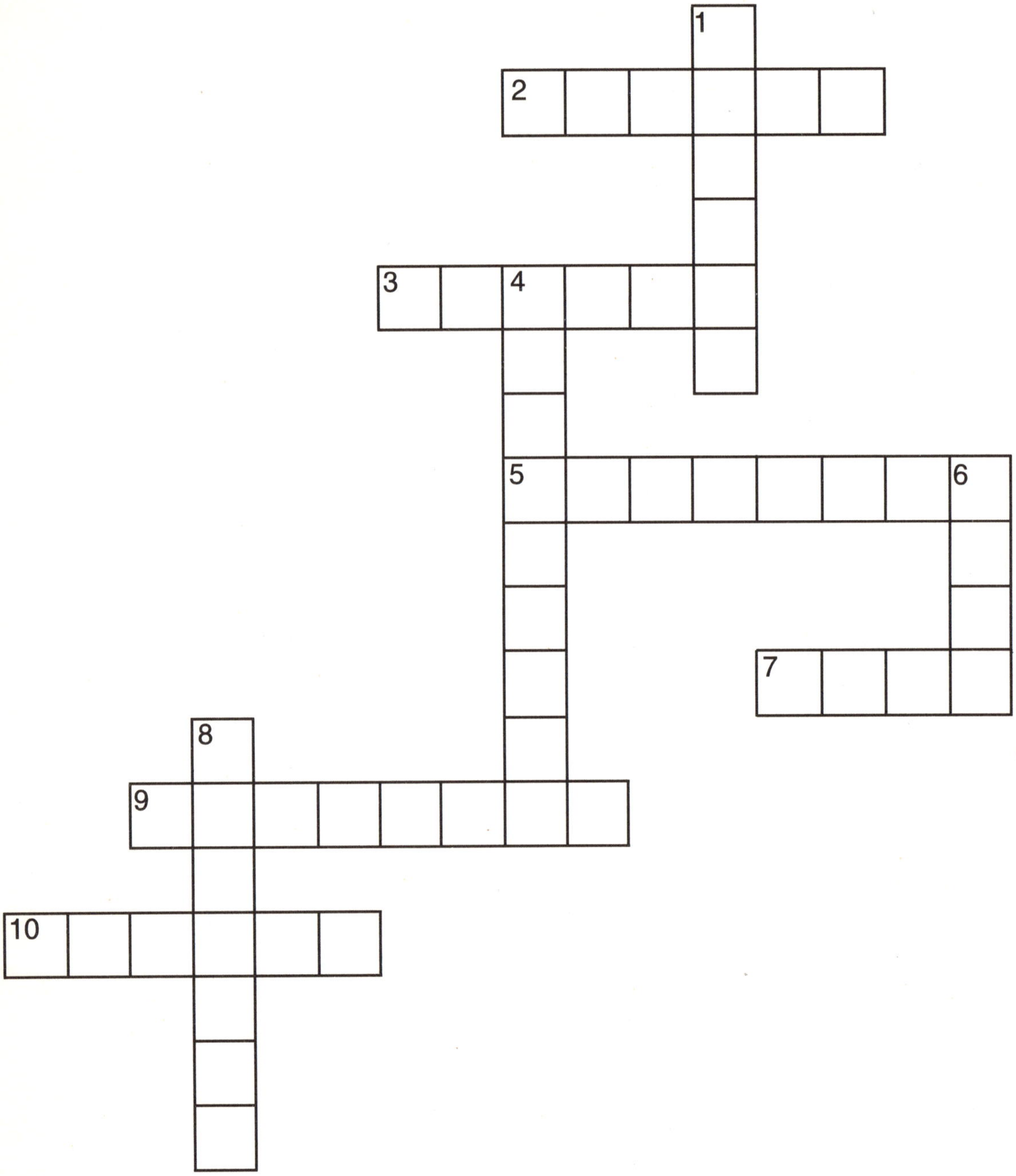

Relationships

Create Your Own Problems

1. Write a word problem involving making a poster in the shape of an octagon.

2. Write a problem about solid figures. Use directions that include stacking and rolling.

3. Write a question about a scalene triangle. Include information about the lengths of the line segments and the measures of the angles.

4. Write a story problem about something in your life that involves parallel lines.

5. Write a question about lines of symmetry. Include a drawing with your question.

Relationships   Name _____   Date _____

Check Your Skills

1. Draw an obtuse angle.

2. Why is the figure at the right not a polygon?

   _____

3. What is the least number of sides a polygon can have?

   _____

4. Can an equilateral triangle be drawn with an obtuse angle? Explain.

   _____

   _____

5. This square has a side 20 centimeters long. Draw a square that is similar to it.

Relationships Name _____ Date _____

Check Your Skills (cont.)

6. How many faces does a triangular pyramid have?

_____

7. Which plane figure is the base of a cylinder?

_____

8. How many lines of symmetry does an equilateral triangle have?

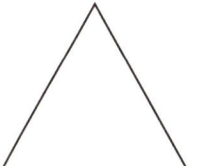

_____

9. Name one solid figure that meets each of these descriptions.
 • can roll
 • can be stacked on top of another object
 • cannot have another object stacked on top of it

_____

10. How many edges does a cube have?

_____

11. Which two vowels in the alphabet have more than one line of symmetry?

A   E   I   O   U

_____

Locations 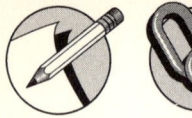    Name _____   Date _____

Going Places

Directions: Use the map to answer the questions.

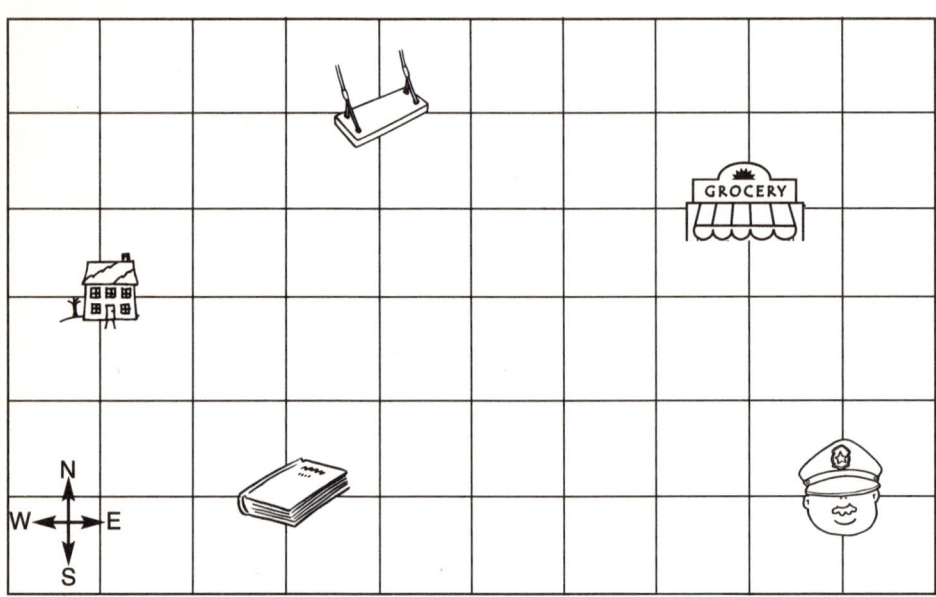

 Park

 School

 Store

 Tara's House

 Police Station

1. Howard leaves the school. He walks north. How many blocks will he walk before he turns right to go to the park? _____

2. Tara leaves the store. She walks west. How many blocks will she walk before she turns left to go to home? _____

3. Chi walks from the store to the park. How many blocks does he walk in all? _____

4. Kim walked 9 blocks to get to the park. From where did Kim walk? _____

THINK

 For questions 1 and 2, explain how you knew which directions were north and west.

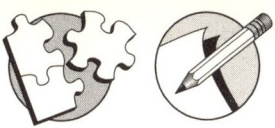

Locations

Name _____ Date _____

Following the Course

Directions: Below is a fitness course. Sam, Elyse, Jon, and Rita are shown in their starting positions. Follow the directions for each person. Identify where each person ends the race.

Sam	**Elyse**	**Jon**	**Rita**
down 5	down 3	down 7	down 3
right 5	right 3	left 2	left 1
up 2	left 2	up 3	right 1
down 4	up 1	right 4	up 2
left 4	right 1	left 3	left 5
down 2	down 7	down 5	down 8

A	**B**	**C**	**D**	**E**	**F**

Sam is at _____ .   **Elyse is at** _____ .   **Jon is at** _____ .   **Rita is at** _____ .

Reveal the Hidden Message

An **ordered pair (x, y)** is a pair of numbers that describes the location of a point. When an ordered pair is graphed on a coordinate grid, the first number, x, tells you how many units to move right (or left) and the second number, y, tells you how many units to move up (or down).

Directions: Color each block on the grid on page 45 that matches the ordered pair listed. The colored blocks will reveal a message.

1. (A, 1), (A, 2), (K, 9), (A, 4), (H, 5), (B, 3), (C, 3), (D, 3), (E, 1), (E, 2), (J, 17), (E, 4), (E, 5)

2. (B, 8), (C, 8), (A, 9), (A, 10), (B, 11), (A, 12), (I, 12), (B, 14), (I, 7), (D, 9), (D, 13), (E, 11)

3. (G, 1), (A, 5), (H, 1), (J, 15), (J, 1), (K, 1), (H, 2), (I, 3), (H, 4), (G, 5), (E, 3), (I, 5), (J, 5), (I, 8)

4. (A, 3), (G, 7), (H, 7), (I, 1), (J, 7), (K, 7), (G, 8), (I, 15), (G, 9), (H, 9), (I, 9), (J, 9)

5. (G, 11), (H, 15), (K, 5), (G, 13), (H, 12), (C, 14), (J, 12), (K, 12)

6. (G, 15), (G, 12), (K, 15), (I, 16), (G, 17), (H, 17), (I, 17), (A, 13), (K, 17)

DO MORE

Make a list of ordered pairs to create your own hidden message. Share your code with a friend.

Reveal the Hidden Message

Directions: Color each block that matches the ordered pairs listed on page 44. After all the blocks are colored, rotate your page clockwise to reveal the message.

Polygon Point Plotting

Directions: Plot the ordered pairs on the grid below. Connect the points to form a polygon.

Ordered pairs: (3, 4), (6, 3), (6, 7), (3, 8)

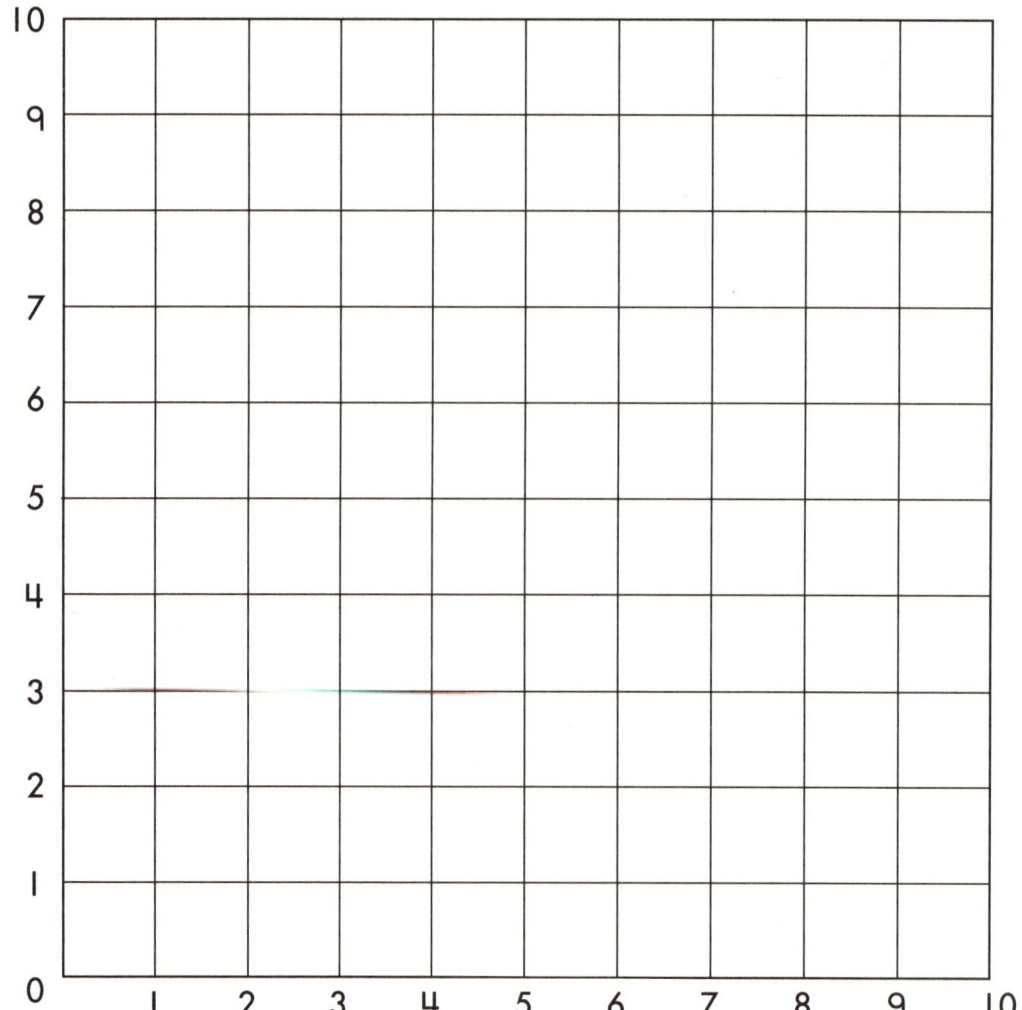

What polygon did you make? _____

Locations

Name the Vertices

Directions: Name the ordered pair for each vertex of the shapes shown.

1.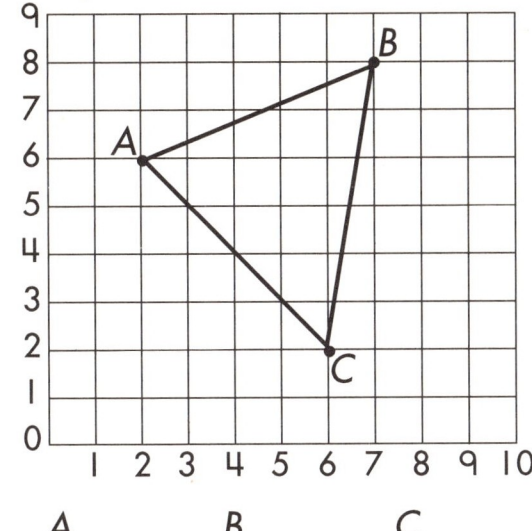

A _____ B _____ C _____

2.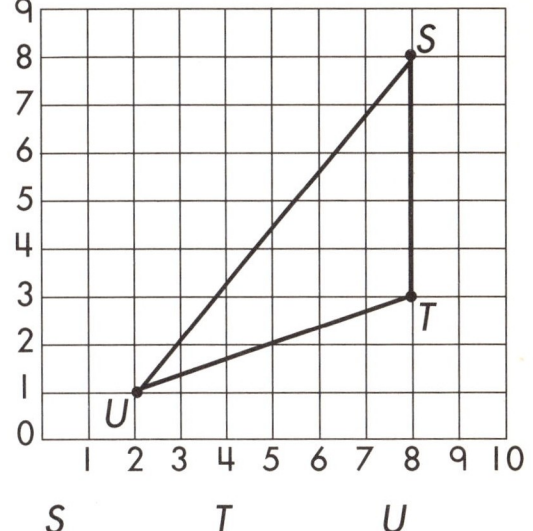

S _____ T _____ U _____

3.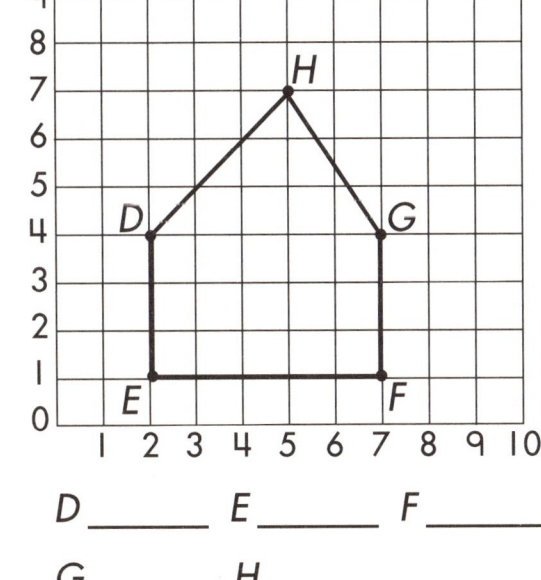

D _____ E _____ F _____

G _____ H _____

4.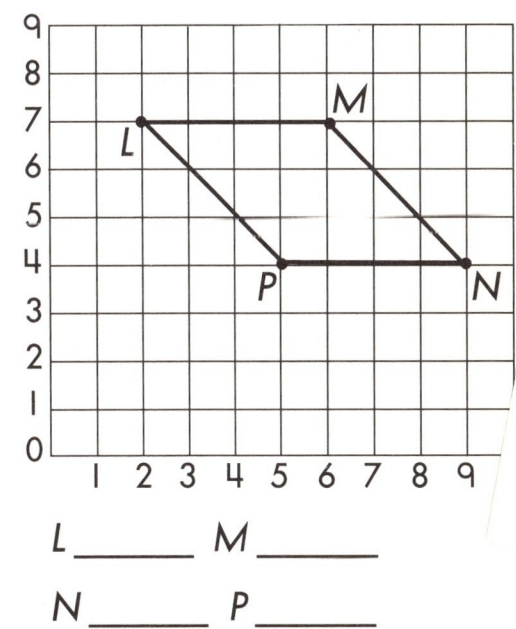

L _____ M _____

N _____ P _____

THINK

Describe how you found the ordered pair for vertex P.

Locations

Name _____ Date _____

Where Is Mr. Smith Going?

Directions: Follow Mr. Smith's steps on the grid below. He starts at the **X**. Name the coordinate where Mr. Smith is when he stops.

1. down 3, right 4
2. up 1, left 5
3. down 6
4. right 4, up 2
5. left 1, down 3
6. left 5, up 6

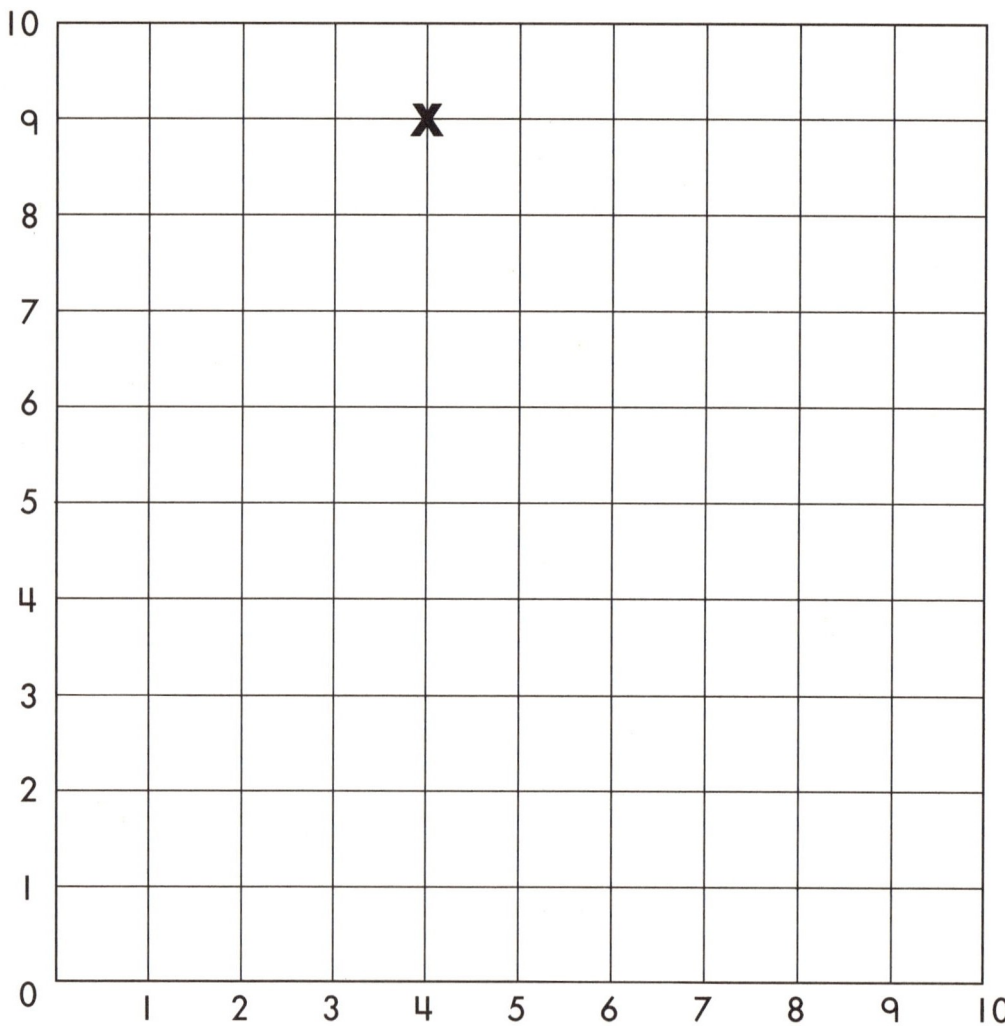

Mr. Smith stopped at point _____.

Locations

Name _____ Date _____

One Point Makes All the Difference

Directions: On each coordinate grid, plot the ordered pairs given. Then connect the points.

Graph A

1. (2, 4)
2. (6, 8)
3. (6, 4)

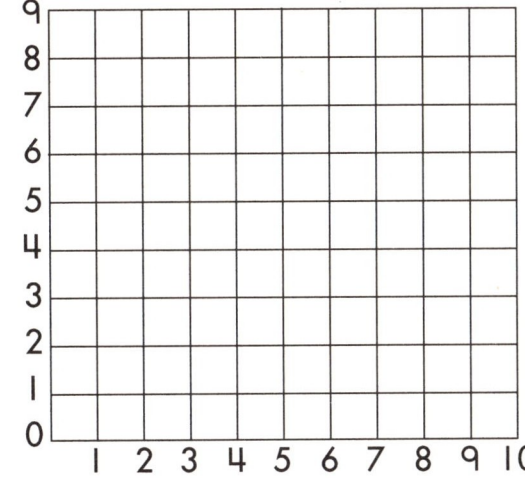

Classify the shape you drew by its angles. _____

Graph B

4. (2, 4)
5. (4, 8)
6. (6, 4)

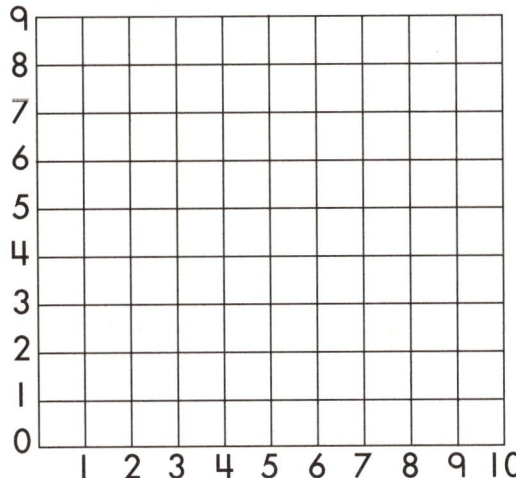

Classify this shape by the lengths of its sides. _____

How did the shape change from Graph A? _____

Locations

Name _____ Date _____

Crazy for Coasters

Directions: Use the diagram of a rollercoaster below to answer the following questions.

1. At which ordered pair is the rollercoaster at its highest point? _____
2. At which ordered pair is the rollercoaster at its lowest point? _____
3. At which ordered pair is the front car of the coaster located? _____
4. At which ordered pair is the back car of the coaster located? _____
5. At the point (17, 7), describe where the front car of the coaster will be?

   _____

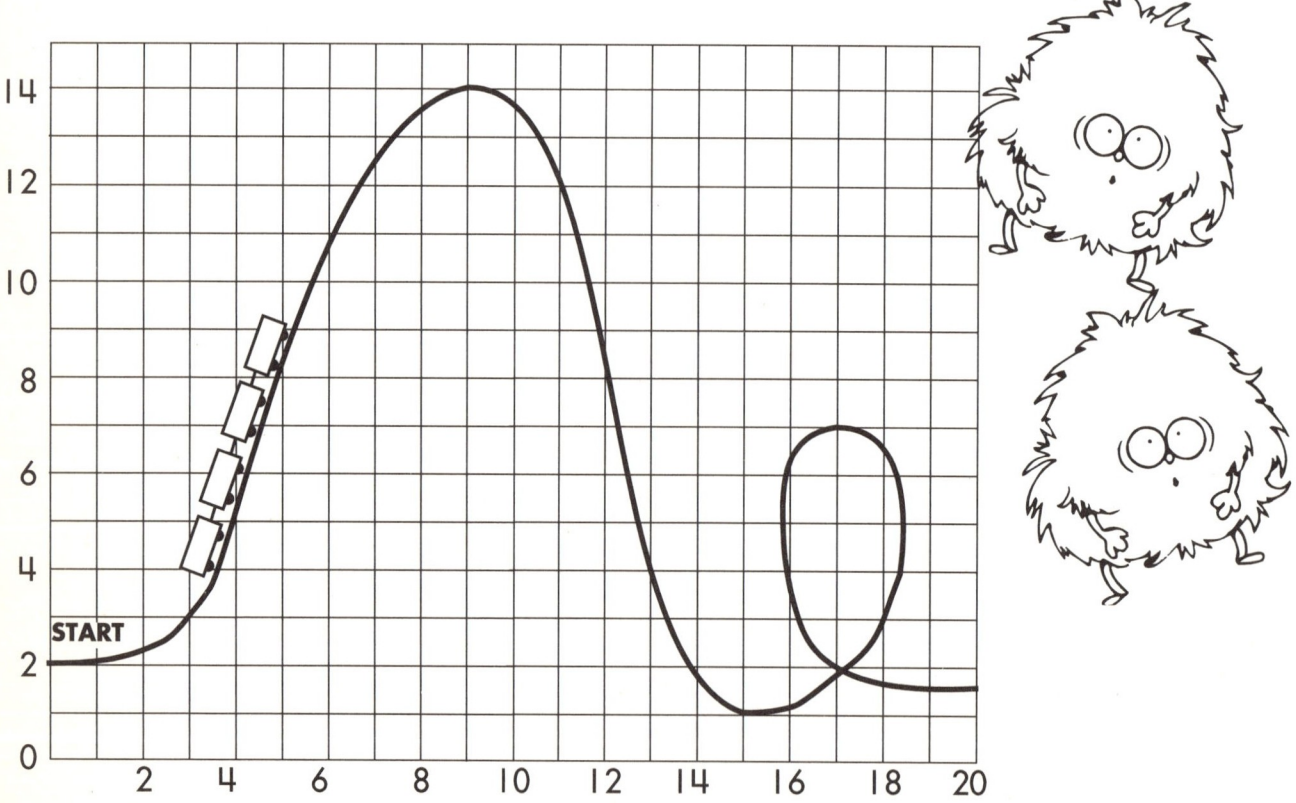

Name _____ Date _____

More About Graphing Points

Directions: Graph the ordered pairs on the coordinate grid below. Then answer the questions that follow.

1. A (5, 6)
2. B (0, 2)
3. C (4, 4)
4. D (1, 9)
5. E (3, 0)
6. F (10, 6)
7. G (7, 2)
8. H (3, 8)
9. J (2, 1)
10. K (6, 1)

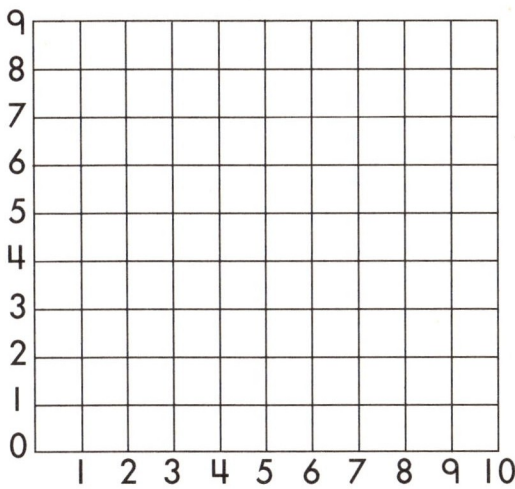

11. Name a point that is to the right of point A.

   _____

12. Name a point that is to the left of point G.

   _____

13. Name a point that is above point J.

   _____

14. Name a point on the same vertical line as point E.

   _____

THINK

Name the coordinates of a possible point W for horizontal line segment AW 4 units long.

Locations Name _____ Date _____

How Far From Point to Point?

Directions: Find the distance (in units) of each line segment on the coordinate grid.

1. $\overline{BC}$ ____

2. $\overline{AB}$ ____

3. $\overline{MN}$ ____

4. $\overline{JK}$ ____

5. $\overline{ST}$ ____

6. $\overline{GH}$ ____

7. $\overline{PM}$ ____

8. $\overline{FG}$ ____

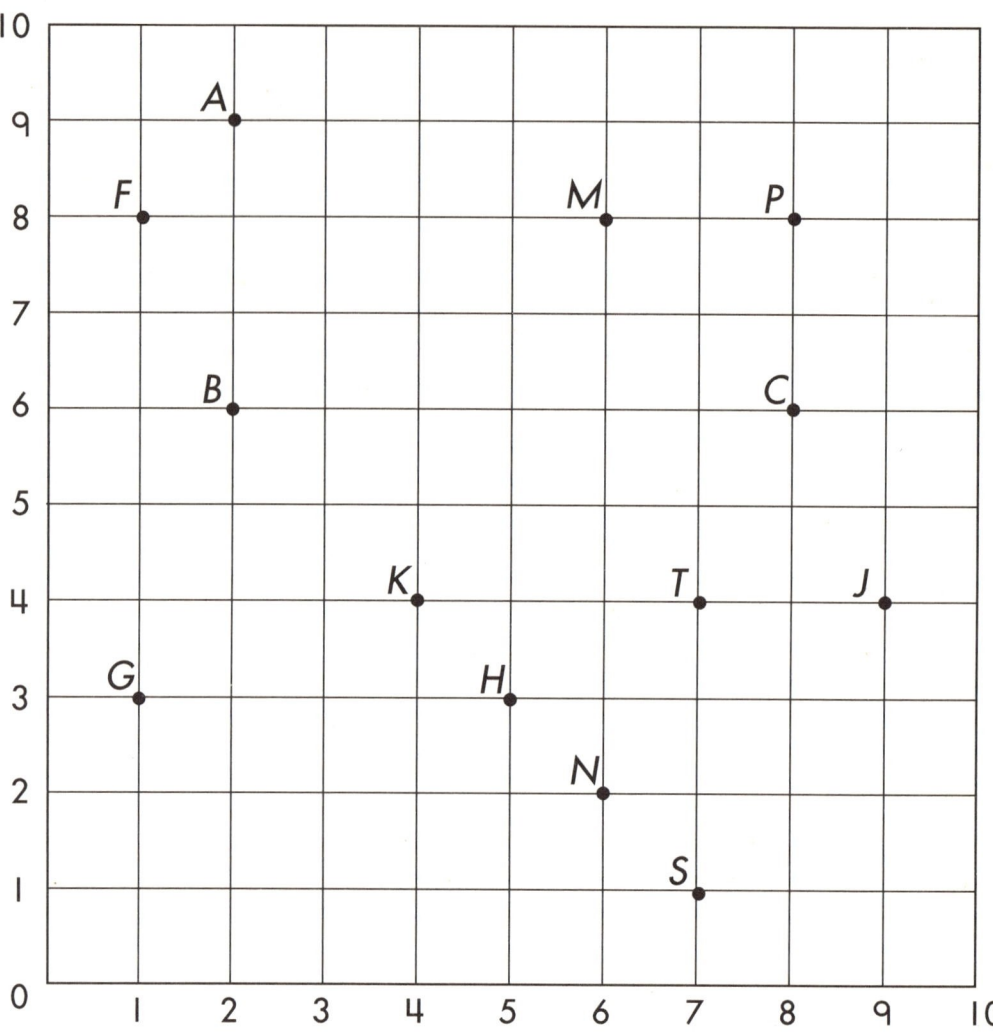

THINK

Draw line segment XY so that it is the same length as line segment GH.
Name the coordinates of the endpoints of a line segment XY.

Locations Name _____ Date _____

Locate the Endpoints

Directions: You are given one endpoint and the length of a line. Use the coordinate grid to help you find the other endpoint for each segment.

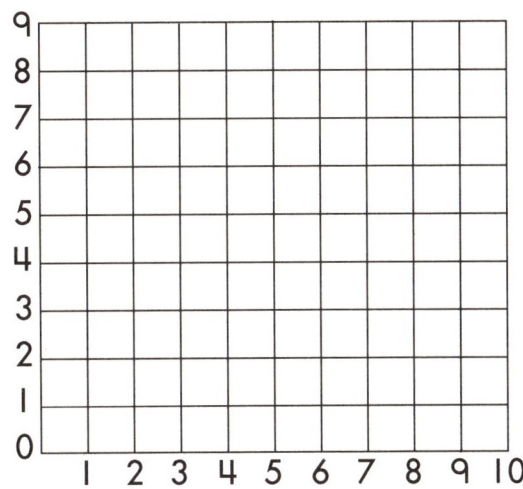

1. Line segment *UV* is a horizontal line 7 units long. Endpoint *U* is at (1, 4). Endpoint *V* is at _____.

2. Line segment *LM* is a vertical line 3 units long. Endpoint *L* is at (0, 2). Endpoint *M* is at _____.

3. Line segment *CD* is a horizontal line 5 units long. Endpoint *C* is at (2, 2). Endpoint *D* is at _____.

4. Line segment *PQ* is a vertical line 4 units long. Endpoint *P* is at (6, 0). Endpoint *Q* is at _____.

5. Line segment *RS* is a vertical line 2.5 units long. Endpoint *R* is at (5, 5). Endpoint *S* is at _____.

THINK

What coordinate do the endpoints of vertical segments have in common?
What coordinate do the endpoints of horizontal segments have in common?

Locations

Name _____ Date _____

From Here to There

Directions: Answer each question. Use the column letter and row number to name your answer.

	A	B	C
1	✖	◯	✿
2	❄	✔	✏
3	◆	▢	✶

1. The shortest path from ✖ to ✶ goes through _____.

2. The shortest path from ◯ to ▢ goes through _____.

3. The shortest path from ✖ to ✿ goes through _____.

4. The shortest path from ✿ to ✶ goes through _____.

5. Describe a path from ◆ to ✏. _____

6. Describe a path from ◯ to ❄. _____

Locations   Name _____ Date _____

Who Gets There First?

Directions: Use the grid and the compass rose to answer the questions.

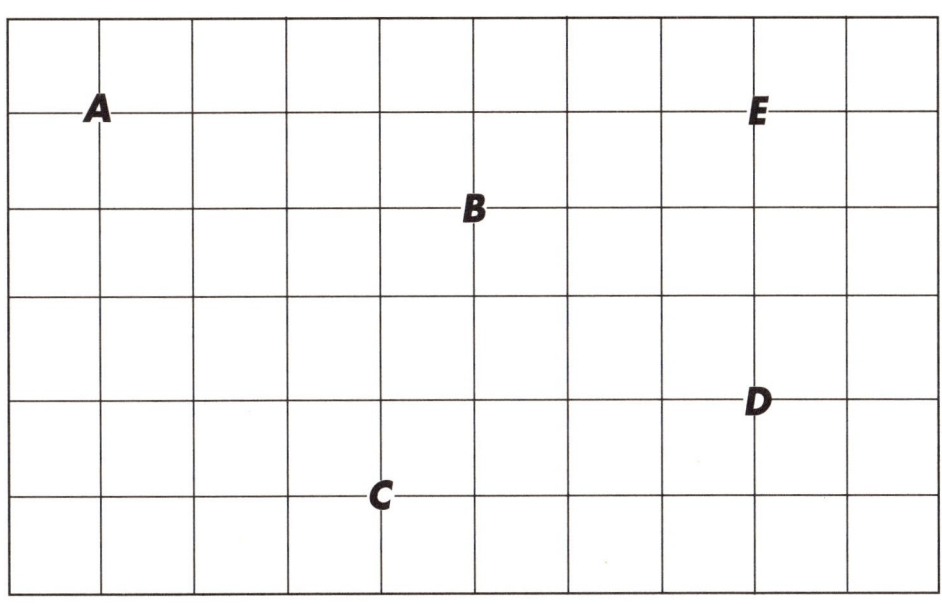

1. Sue and Hector are at point A.
   Sue walks south, then east to get to point C.
   Hector walks southeast to get to point C.
   Who walks the shortest distance? _____

2. Abbey and Tim are at point D.
   Abbey walks northwest to get to point B.
   Tim walks north, then west to get to point B.
   Who walks the shortest distance? _____

3. Dean is at point A. He walks south, then east to point B
   Eve is a point D. She walks west, then south to point C.
   Who walks the shortest distance? _____

THINK

For each person that walked one direction and then turned to walk a different direction, what type of angle did they make when they turned?

55

Published by Instructional Fair. Copyright protected.   0-7424-2983-0 *Using the Standards: Geometry*

Locations

Making a Course

Directions: Work with a partner to create a coordinate grid course.

Select a partner. Choose a location where you can make a 10 step by 10 step grid. (If you are in a room with a tile floor, the tiles can be your grid.)

Choose a point to be the origin. Use masking tape to mark 10 units to the right of the origin and 10 units up from the origin.

You can use a marker to write on the masking tape to label the units.

Work separately from your partner to create a course for your partner. Include directions for the following:

1. the ordered pair where to start

2. a move to make, such as right 3, up 1

3. a turn to make, either a quarter turn, half turn, or full turn (Include clockwise or counterclockwise.)

4. another move to make

5. another turn to make

6. another move to make (Be sure you know where your partner should be at the end of your course. Do not share it.)

Take turns following each other's courses.

Check that your partner followed the directions and ended at the correct point.

Locations Name _____ Date _____

Carving a Jack-o-Lantern

Directions: Draw a face on the pumpkin below.
List the ordered pairs that outline each eye, the nose, and mouth.

Left Eye _____   **Right Eye** _____

Nose _____   **Mouth** _____

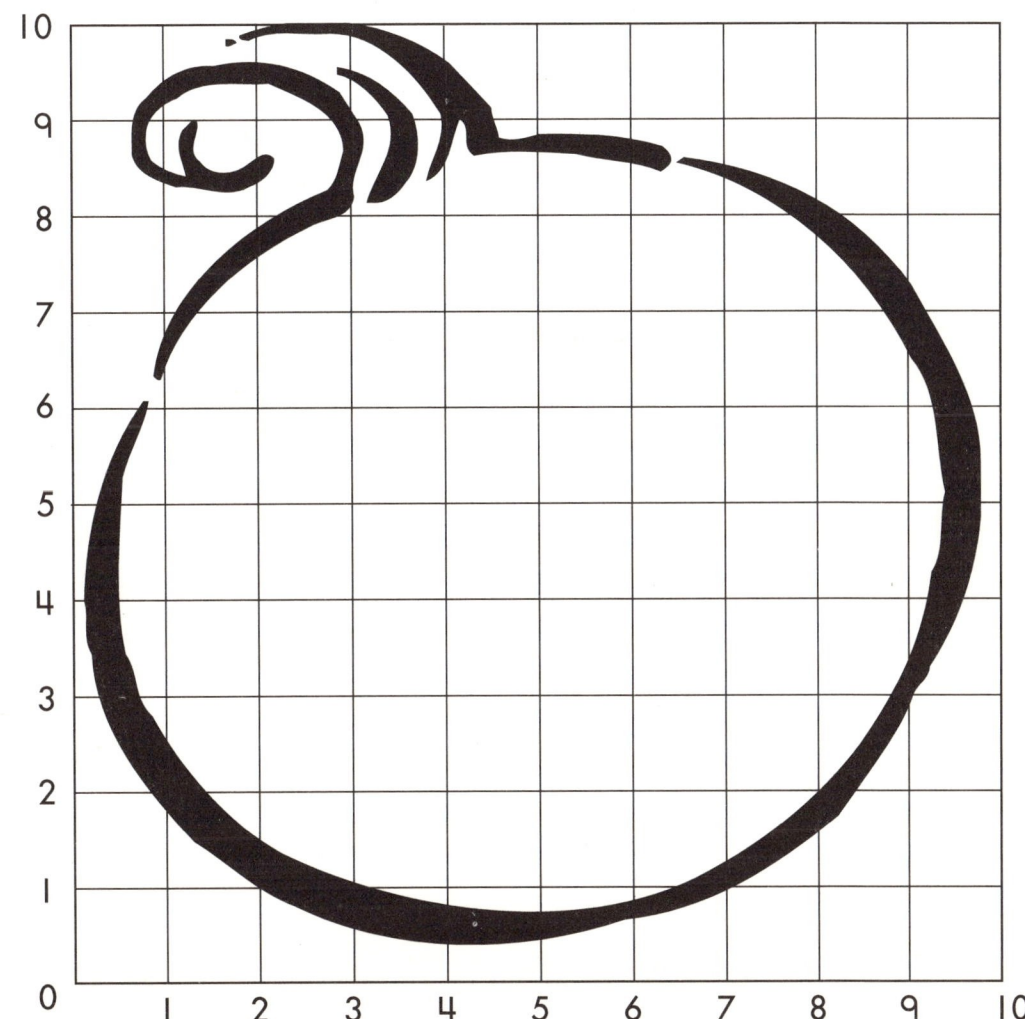

57

Published by Instructional Fair. Copyright protected.   0-7424-2983-0 *Using the Standards: Geometry*

Name _____ Date _____

Drawing Lines of Symmetry

A **line of symmetry** is a line that divides a picture or shape into two equal halves. Each half a mirror image of the other half. A line of symmetry can be vertical, horizontal, or diagonal.

A square has 4 lines of symmetry.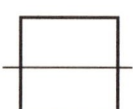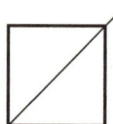

Directions: Draw the line or lines of symmetry for each shape.

1.

2.

3.

4.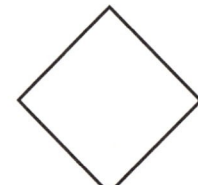

5.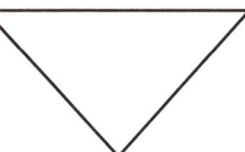

6.

DO MORE

 Draw a shape that does not have a line of symmetry.

Locations

Create with Symmetry

Directions: The points on the left side of a picture are shown. The picture has a line of symmetry shown with a dotted line. Place the points on the right half of the picture. Connect the points to draw the picture.

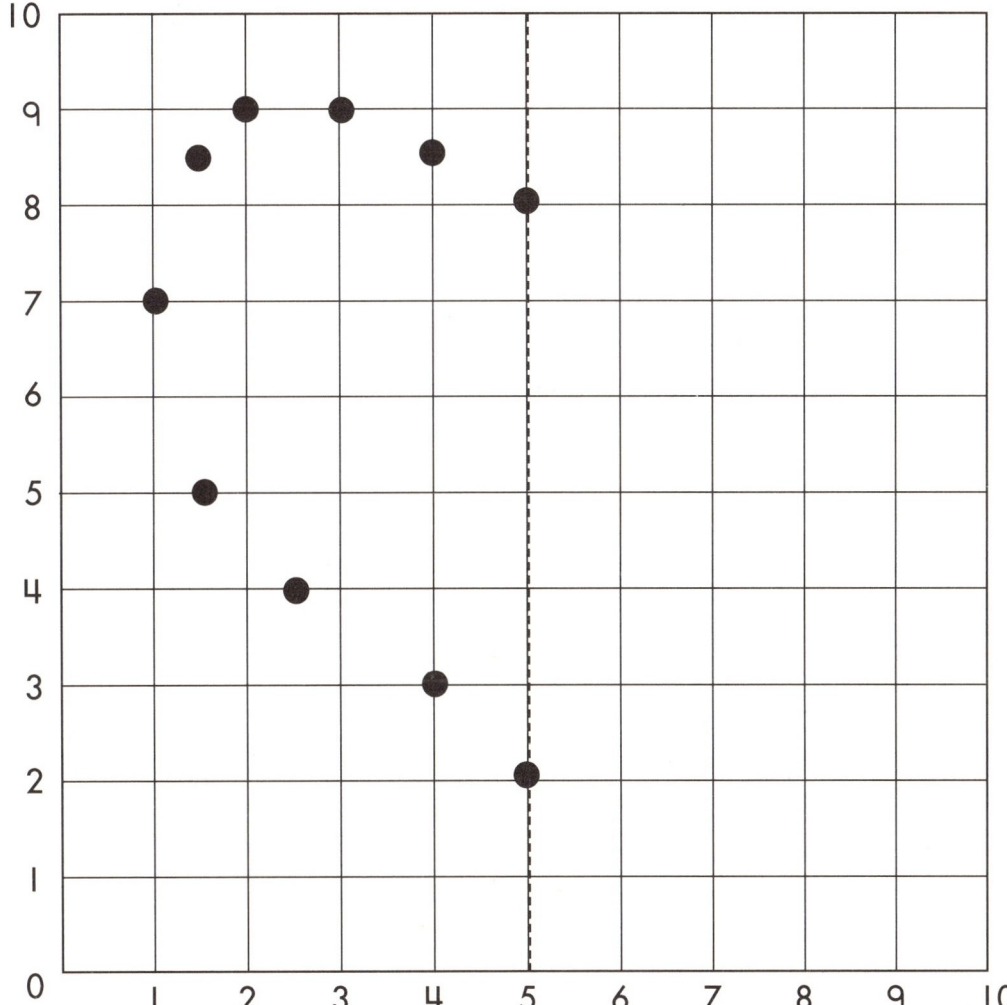

Name the ordered pairs you graphed on the right side of the picture.

1. _____   2. _____   3. _____   4. _____

5. _____   6. _____   7. _____   8. _____

Locations

Reflect Each Other

Directions: Work in a group of three to create a coordinate grid.

Choose a location where you can make a 10 step by 10 step grid. (If you are in a room with a tile floor, the tiles can be your grid.)

Choose a point to be the origin. Use masking tape to mark 10 units to the right of the origin and 10 units up from from the origin.

You can use a marker to write on the masking tape to label the units.

Mark a line on the grid as a line a symmetry.

Each person needs paper and markers.

Use the line of symmetry to name points that are reflections of each other.

1. The first person chooses a point on the coordinate grid and writes the ordered pair on a piece of paper, large enough to be seen from a distance. Stand on that point on the coordinate grid, and show your ordered pair.

2. A second person goes to a point on the opposite side of the line of symmetry that is a reflection of the first person's point. Write the ordered pair on a piece of paper, large enough to be seen from a distance. Stand on that point on the coordinate grid and show your ordered pair.

3. The third person needs to decide if the points are equal distances from the line of symmetry and are reflections of each other. If not, the three people need to work together until they all agree that the points are reflections of each other.

Repeat Steps 1 - 3 until everyone has had a turn to play each role in the game.

Locations   Name _____   Date _____

Look in the Mirror

Directions: Complete the missing half of the picture so that the two halves are symmetrical.
Use the grid to help you.

1.

2.

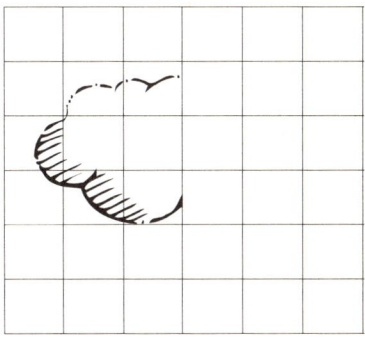

3.

4.

THINK

How does the grid help you complete the missing half of the picture?

Published by Instructional Fair. Copyright protected.   0-7424-2983-0 *Using the Standards: Geometry*

Locations

Create Your Own Problems

1. Write a question about ordered pairs on a coordinate grid.

2. Draw a polygon on a coordinate grid. Label the vertices with letters. Write a question that asks about a specific vertex.

3. Draw a coordinate grid map of a town. Locate places in the town on the grid. Write questions about the locations of the places in the town.

4. Write a question about symmetry that involves a picture on a coordinate grid.

5. Use ordered pairs and grid paper to make a puzzle that reveals a hidden message.

Locations

Name _____ Date _____

Check Your Skills

Use the coordinate grid below for questions 1 and 2.

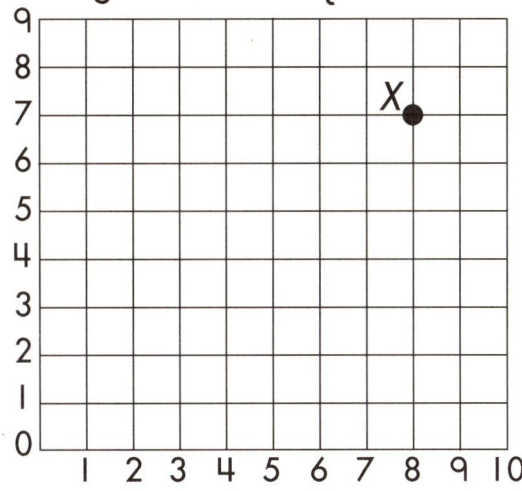

1. Name the coordinate of point X. _____

2. Graph the ordered pairs (2, 2), (2, 5), and (5, 2). Name the fourth ordered pair that completes the graph of a square.

   _____

3. Graph the ordered pairs (4, 5), (7, 8), (4, 3), and (7, 3). Then connect the points. Which shape did you make?

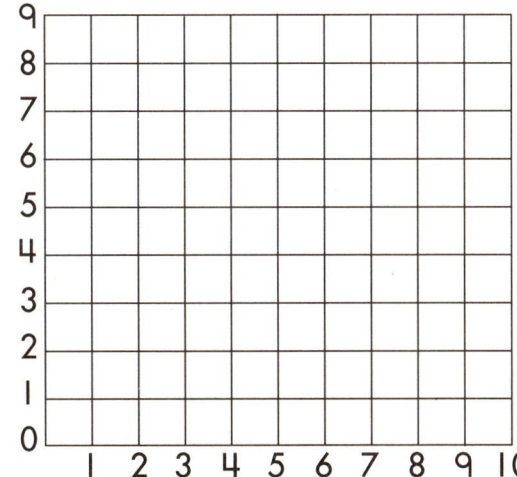

_____

Locations

Check Your Skills (cont.)

Use the coordinate grid below for questions 4 - 7.

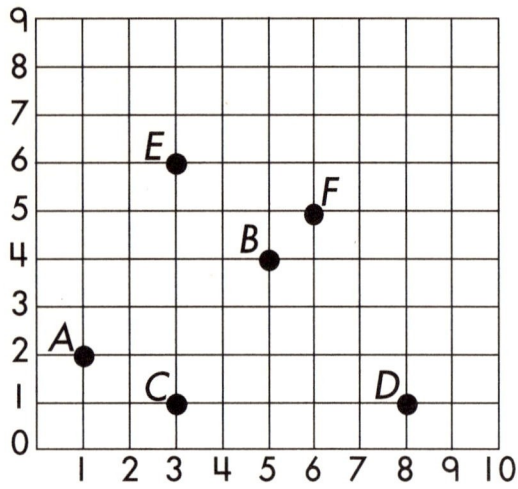

4. Which point is to the left of point C and below point B?

   _____

5. Which point is above and to the right of point B?

   _____

6. What is the distance between point C and point D?

   _____

7. Describe how to move from point E to point F.

   _____

Transformations

Name _____ **Date** _____

Flips, Slides, and Turns

A **flip** is a transformation that creates a mirror image of the original image.

A horizontal flip is a flip across a vertical line.

A vertical flip is a flip across a horizontal line.

A **slide** is a transformation that creates an image moved from the location of the original image.

A **turn** is a transformation that creates a rotated image of the original image.

horizontal flip

vertical flip

Directions: Draw what each shape looks like when the named transformation is applied.

1. Flip

2. Slide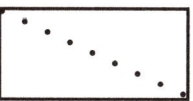

3. Turn (quarter turn clockwise)

4. Flip

Transformations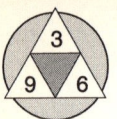

Match the Transformation

Directions: Circle the picture that shows the named transformation.

1. Flip   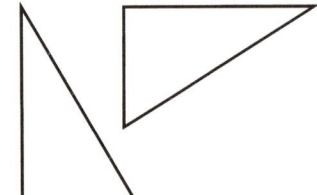   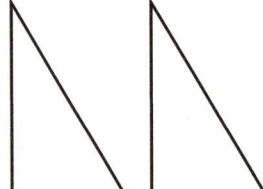   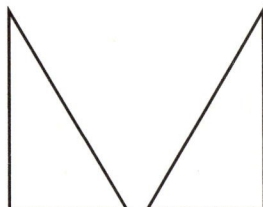

2. Slide          

3. Turn          

4. Turn         

5. Slide   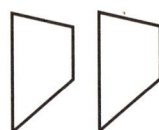      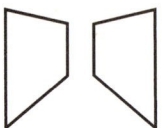

Transformations     Name _____   Date _____

Are You Seeing Double?

Directions: Decide if the pairs of figures are congruent. Write yes or no. If yes, tell what transformation is shown.

1.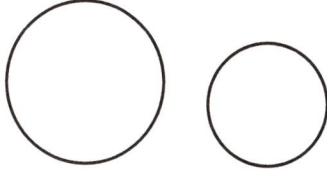

   _____

2.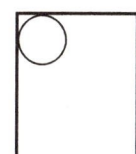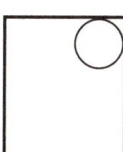

   _____

3.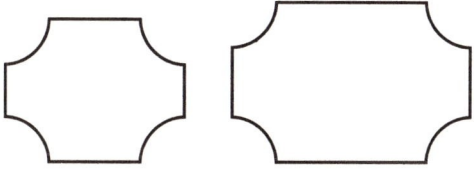

   _____

4.

   _____

5.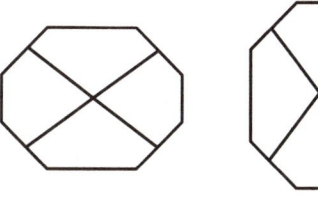

   _____

6.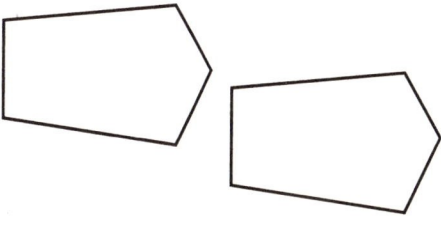

   _____

Name ______________________ Date ______________

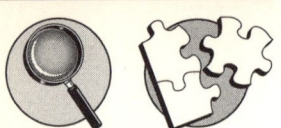

Slide from Start to Finish

Directions: Begin at START. Find a path to the FINISH by connecting the moons that used a slide to get to its next location. You can slide left, right, up, or down. If a moon used a flip or turn to get to its next location, it is NOT part of the path to the FINISH.

START

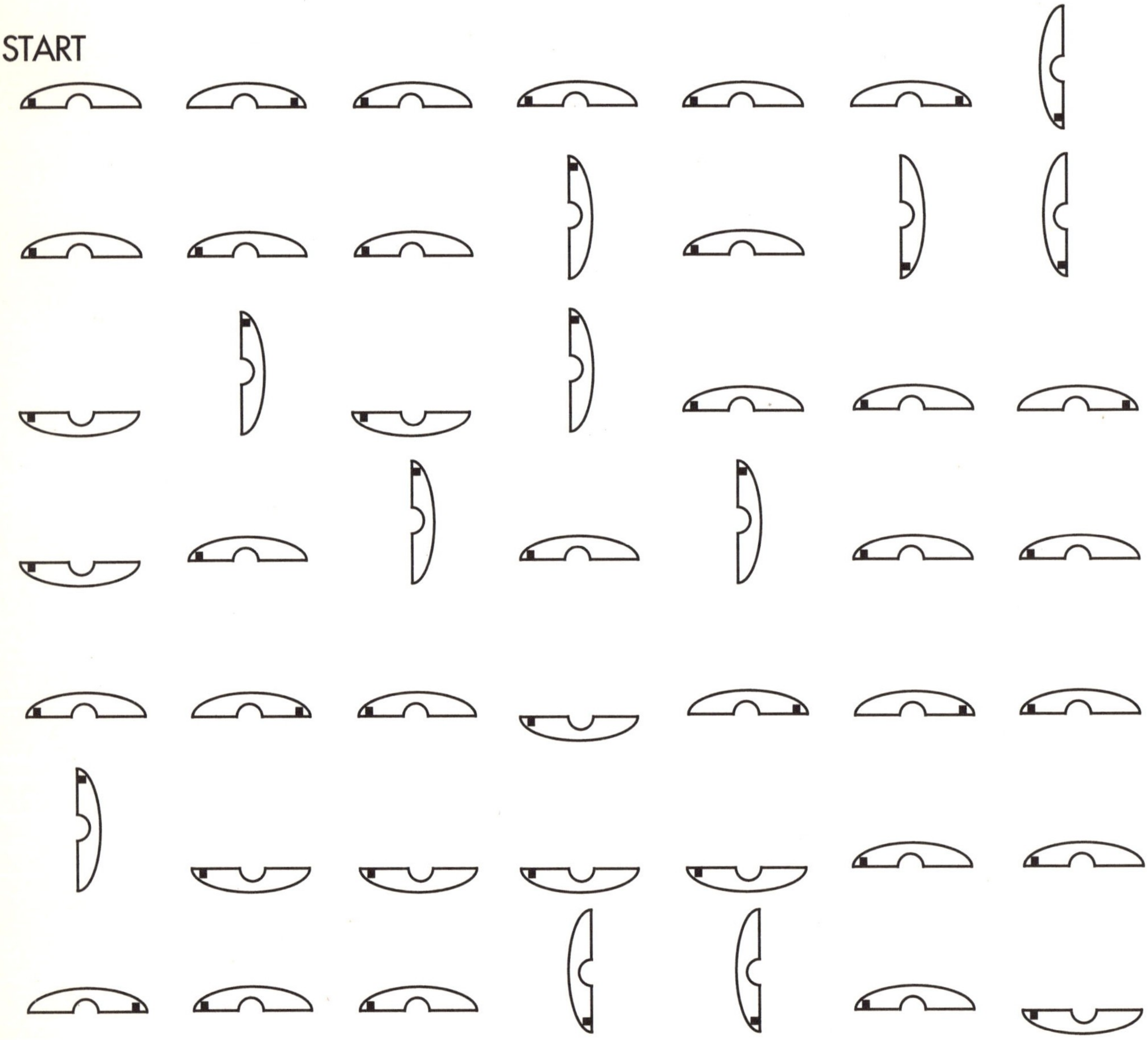

FINISH

0-7424-2983-0 *Using the Standards: Geometry*

Transformations

Name _____ Date _____

Transforming Letters

Directions: Make each set of transformations for the given letter. Use the transformed letter to the left of each space to make the next transformation. Make the turns a quarter turn clockwise. Make the flips over a vertical line.

1. **E** _____ _____ _____ _____ _____
       flip   turn   flip   turn   flip

2. **V** _____ _____ _____ _____ _____
       slide   turn   flip   slide   turn

3. **A** _____ _____ _____ _____ _____
       turn   turn   flip   flip   slide

4. **N** _____ _____ _____ _____ _____
       flip   flip   slide   turn   turn

THINK

For which letters was the result of a slide the same as the result of a flip?

Published by Instructional Fair. Copyright protected.   0-7424-2983-0 *Using the Standards: Geometry*

Transforming a Clown

Directions: Help this clown find his way out of the path of transformation. Sketch the transformation of the clown's face in each square. Name the last transformation.

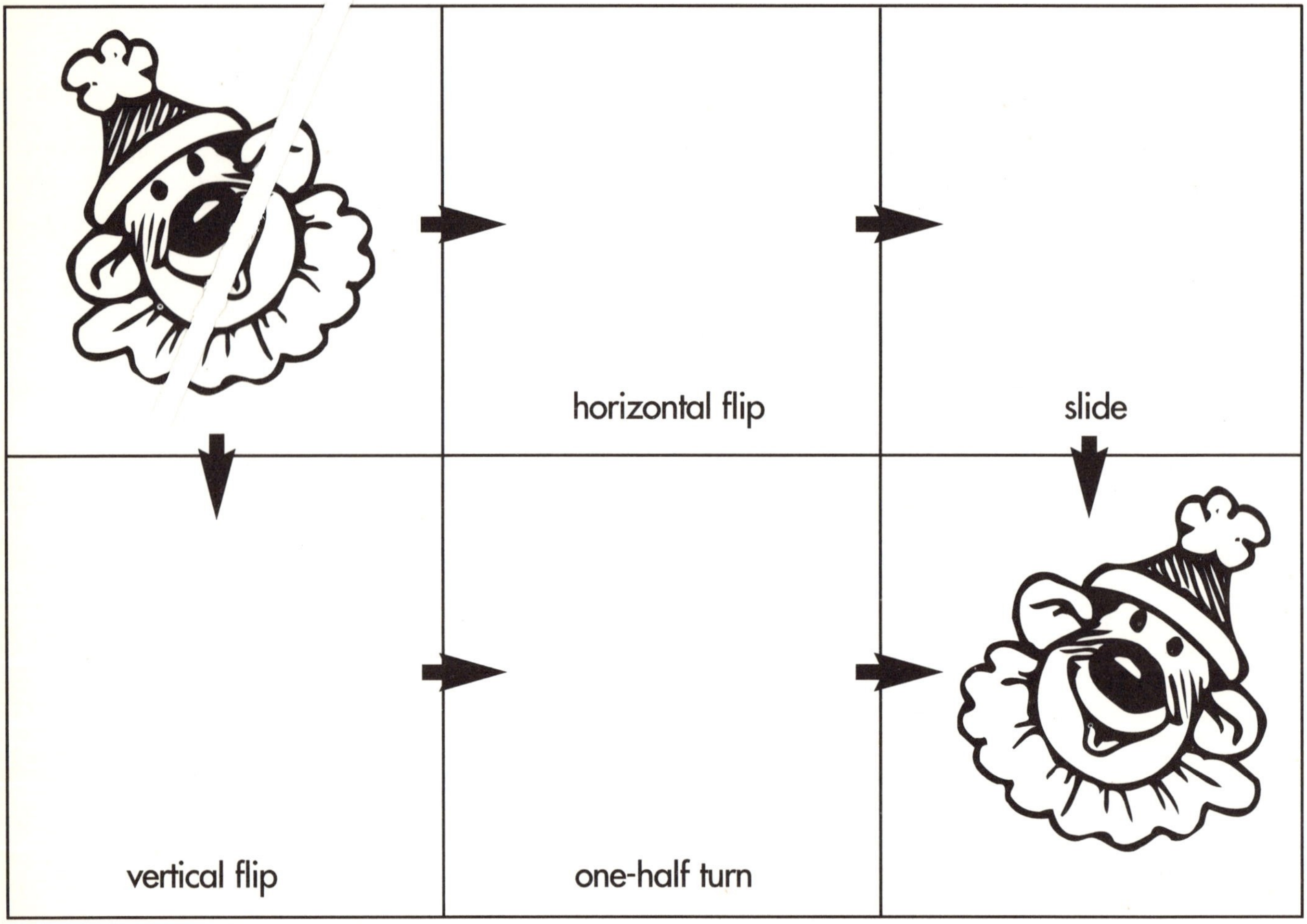

	horizontal flip	slide
vertical flip	one-half turn	

_____

Transformations

Name _____ Date _____

Transforming Letters

Directions: Make each set of transformations for the given letter. Use the transformed letter to the left of each space to make the next transformation. Make the turns a quarter turn clockwise. Make the flips over a vertical line.

1. E _____ _____ _____ _____ _____
        flip   turn   flip   turn   flip

2. V _____ _____ _____ _____ _____
        slide   turn   flip   slide   turn

3. A _____ _____ _____ _____ _____
        turn   turn   flip   flip   slide

4. N _____ _____ _____ _____ _____
        flip   flip   slide   turn   turn

THINK

For which letters was the result of a slide the same as the result of a flip?

Transforming a Clown

Directions: Help this clown find his way out of the path of transformation. Sketch the transformation of the clown's face in each square. Name the last transformation.

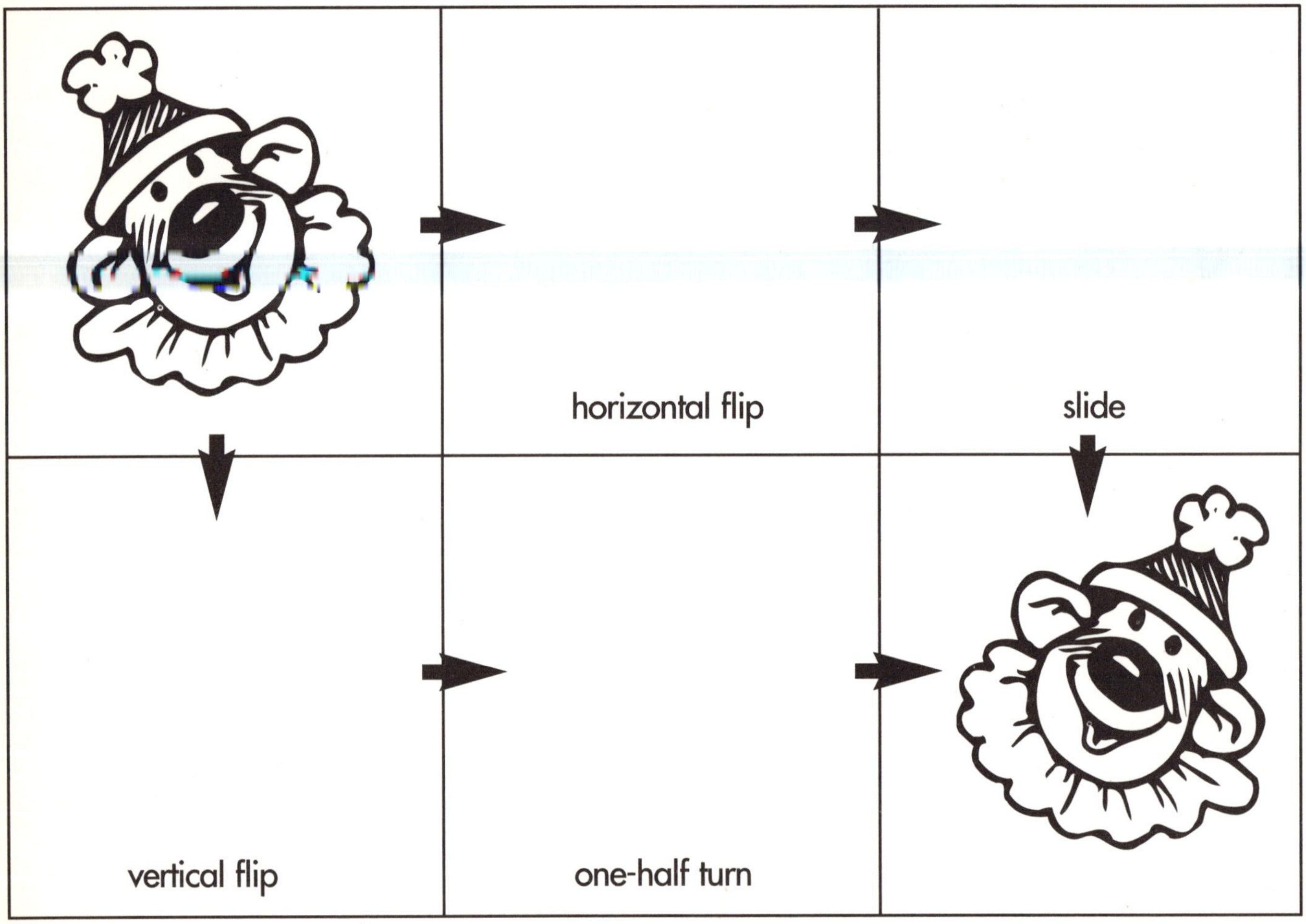

	horizontal flip	slide
vertical flip	one-half turn	

_____

Transformations   Name _____   Date _____

Letter Look Alikes

Directions: Put a ◯ around the flipped letters.
Put a ☐ around the turned letters
Put a △ around the slid letters.

1. ⌐ (flipped L)

2. F

3. ⊥ (upside-down T)

4. U

5. Ò (upside-down Q)

6. a (rotated)

7. ⌒ (rotated J)

8. D

9. w (rotated)

10. i

11. ʎ (upside-down y)

12. H (rotated)

THINK

For which letters did you put both a circle and a triangle around?

71

Published by Instructional Fair. Copyright protected.
0-7424-2983-0 *Using the Standards: Geometry*

Name ____________________ Date ______________

Create Congruent Figures

Directions: Create 3 congruent figures for each figure shown using a slide, flip, and turn. Use the original image for each transformation.

	Slide	Horizontal Flip	Clockwise Turn
1. 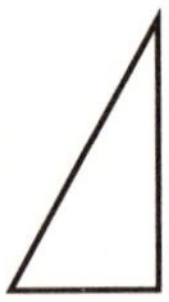	________	________	________
2. 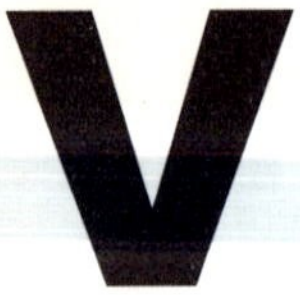	________	________	________
3. 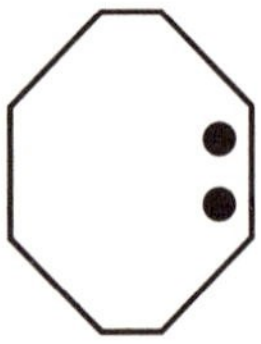	________	________	________
4. 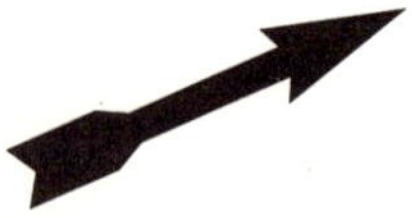	________	________	________
5. 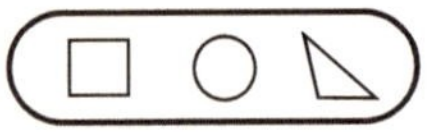	________	________	________

0-7424-2983-0 *Using the Standards: Geometry*

Transformations Name _____ Date _____

Moving to the Next Location

Directions: For each transformation named, label as slide, horizontal flip, vertical flip, or turn.

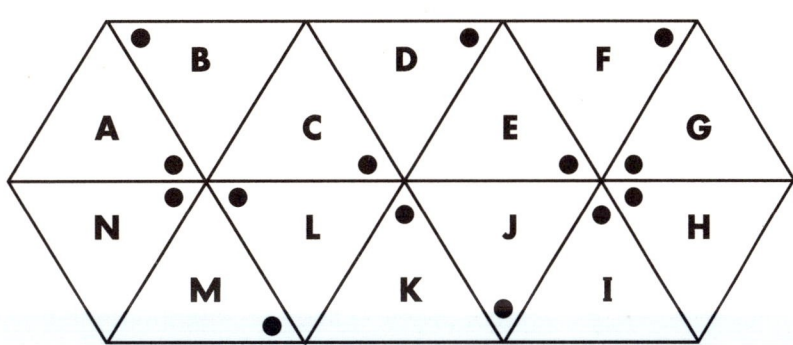

1. A to C _____

2. A to N _____

3. A to G _____

4. C to E _____

5. D to F _____

6. G to K _____

7. K to E _____

8. M to C _____

9. G to H _____

10. I to H _____

Transformations   Name _____ Date _____

Lines of Symmetry

Directions: Decide if the line shown is a line of symmetry. Write yes or no in the blank.

1.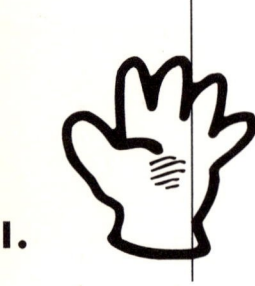

   _____

2.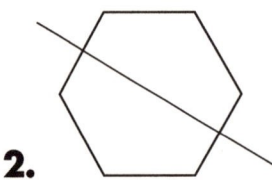

   _____

3.

   _____

4.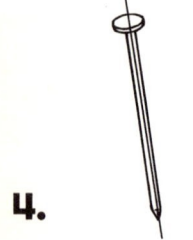

   _____

5.

   _____

6.

   _____

THINK

 Choose a picture that does not have a line of symmetry. Explain why it did not have a line of symmetry.

Transformations     Name _____   Date _____

Many Lines of Symmetry

Directions: Circle the number of lines of symmetry for each figure shown.

1. 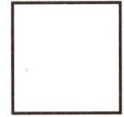   0   1   2   3   4

2.    0   1   2   3   4

3.    0   1   2   3   4

4.    0   1   2   3   4

5.    0   1   2   3   4

6. 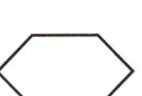   0   1   2   3   4

7.    0   1   2   3   4

Transformations

Name _____ Date _____

Point Symmetry

A figure that is turned about a point and looks exactly like itself before one complete rotation (360 degrees) has **point symmetry**.

Point symmetry is also called **rotational symmetry**.

Directions: Decide if the figure has point symmetry. Write yes or no.

1.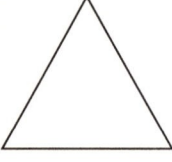

   _____

2.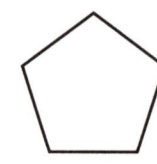

   _____

3.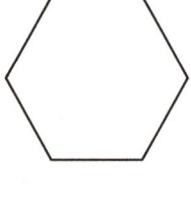

   _____

4.

   _____

5.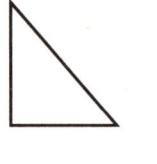

   _____

6.

   _____

Pictures with Point Symmetry

Directions: Draw each picture after it is turned one-quarter turn clockwise about the point shown.

1.

•

2.

•

Transformations    Name _____ Date _____

Arrange Flowers

Directions: Add at least four more flowers to the vase below. Each flower should be a slide, flip, or turn of the flower that is in the vase.

DO MORE

 Tell how many flowers you added that are flip transformations.
Tell how many flowers you added that are slide transformations.
Tell how many flowers you added that are turn transformations.
Which transformation was the easiest to draw? Explain.

Transformations

Create Your Own Problems

1. Write a problem that involves turning the minute hand of a clock.

2. Write a pattern question that includes flip transformations. Draw at least five shapes of your pattern.

3. Write a word problem about how a slide transformation is used in sports.

4. Write a problem that includes two different transformations.

5. Make a question about a plane figure that has 4 lines of symmetry.

6. Make a question about a solid figure and lines of symmetry. Include a drawing with your question.

Transformations

Check Your Skills

1. Name two letters of the alphabet that can be flipped and will still look the same.

   _____

2. How many lines of symmetry does a regular pentagon have?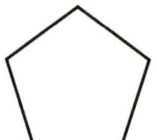

   _____

3. Which transformation creates a mirror image of the original image?

   _____

4. Which transformation is shown below?

   _____

5. Make a core for a pattern by flipping the shape below vertically, then sliding it twice.

    _____   _____   _____

Transformations Name _____ Date _____

Check Your Skills (cont.)

6. Sketch the figure below after a horizontal flip.

7. How many lines of symmetry are in the figure below? Draw the lines of symmetry.

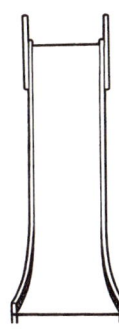

8. Does the shape below have point symmetry?

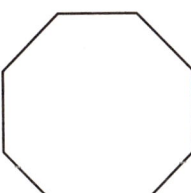

9. Describe how the letter "b" can be transformed to make the the following.

    a. letter "d" _____

    b. letter "p" _____

Modeling     Name _____   Date _____

Shape Scavenger Hunt

Directions: Shapes are all around. Go on a shape hunt to find these shapes in your house. Name the room where you found each shape. Describe the object you found.

1. square _____

2. octagon _____

3. trapezoid _____

4. triangle _____

5. rectangle _____

6. pentagon _____

7. right triangle _____

8. hexagon _____

9. parallelogram _____

10. equilateral triangle _____

THINK

 What shape took you the longest amount of time to find?

Published by Instructional Fair. Copyright protected.   0-7424-2983-0 *Using the Standards: Geometry*

Modeling   Name _____ Date _____

Patterns of Shapes

Directions: Look at each pattern. Draw the next three shapes in the pattern.

1.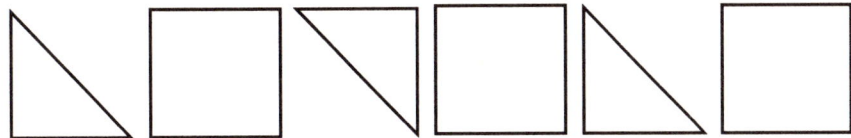

2.

3.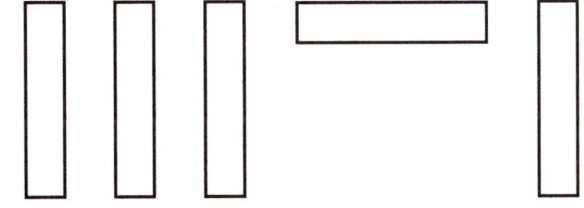

4.

THINK

Which pattern above is made with the transformation of one shape?
Which pattern above is made with the transformation of two shapes?

Use Dot Paper to Draw

Directions: Use the dot paper to draw each figure named.

1. square
2. right triangle
3. rectangle
4. parallelogram

THINK

Why is dot paper useful for drawing figures?

Modeling

Name _____ Date _____

Isosceles Drawings

Directions: Use the dot paper to draw each figure named.

1. isosceles triangle
2. isosceles trapezoid

THINK

How do you know that your figures are isosceles without using a ruler?

Name ______________________ Date ______________

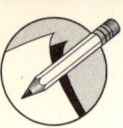

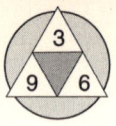

Triangle Types

Directions: Draw each triangle named.

1. right triangle

2. acute triangle

3. isosceles triangle

4. scalene triangle

5. obtuse triangle

6. equilateral triangle

0-7424-2983-0 *Using the Standards: Geometry*

Draw Quadrilaterals

Directions: Draw each quadrilateral named.

1. rectangle

2. trapezoid

3. parallelogram

4. square

5. rhombus

6. isosceles trapezoid

THINK

 Which shapes named above are not parallelograms?

Modeling

Solid Figure Scavenger Hunt

Directions: Solid figures are all around. Go on another shape hunt to find these solid figures in your house. Name the room where you find the solid figure. Describe each solid figure.

1. cone _____

2. cylinder _____

3. cube _____

4. square pyramid _____

5. rectangular prism _____

6. triangular prism _____

7. sphere _____

8. triangular pyramid _____

THINK

Which solid figure that you found was most unusual?

Modeling   Name _____ Date _____

Rectangular Prism Dot-to-Dot

Directions: Follow the steps, and learn how to draw a rectangular prism.

```
            5•                           •8


  1•                     •4



            6•                           •7



  2•                     •3
```

Use solid line segments for Steps 1 - 3.

Step 1: Connect dots 1 to 2, 2 to 3, 3 to 4, and 4 to 1.

Step 2: Connect dots 5 to 8 and 8 to 7.

Step 3: Connect dots 1 to 5, 4 to 8, and 3 to 7.

Use dashed line segments for Step 4.

Step 4: Connect dots 5 to 6, 2 to 6, and 6 to 7.

DO MORE

   Draw a cube on your own.

Modeling   Name _____ Date _____

Square Pyramid Dot-to-Dot

Directions: Follow the steps, and learn how to draw a square pyramid.

•5

1•   •4

2•   •3

Use solid line segments for Steps 1 - 3.
     Step 1: Connect dots 1 to 2, 2 to 3, and 3 to 4.
     Step 2: Connect dots 5 to 1 and 5 to 4.
     Step 3: Connect dots 5 to 2 and 5 to 3.
Use dashed line segments for Step 4.
     Step 4: Connect dots 1 to 4.

DO MORE

Draw a triangular pyramid on your own.

Name _____ Date _____

Face by Face

Directions: Use the model of each solid figure to name the number of its faces.

1.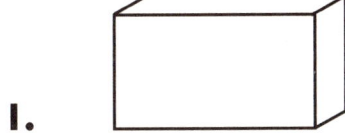

2.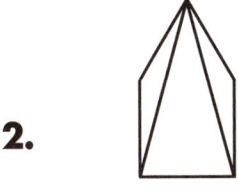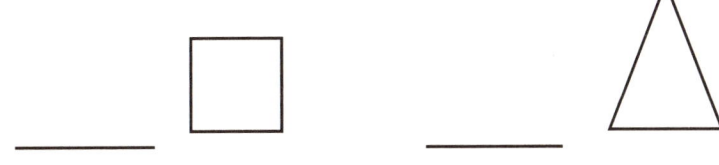

3.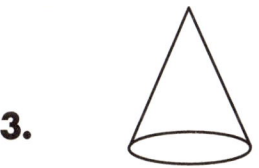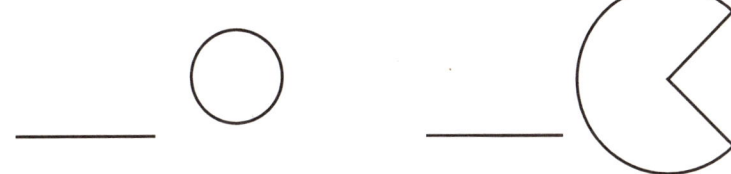

4.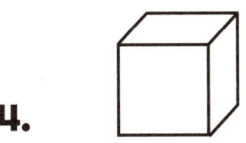

5.

| Modeling | Name _____ Date _____ |

The Face That Does Not Belong

Directions: Place an X over the solid figure that cannot have the shape shown in the left column as one of its faces.

1.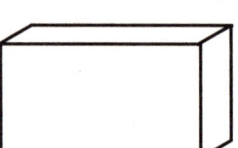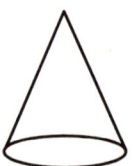

2.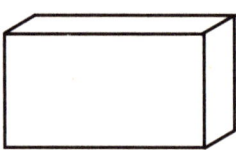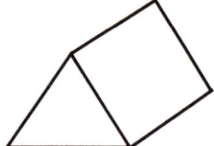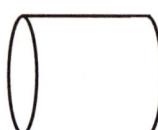

3.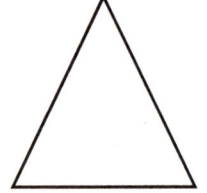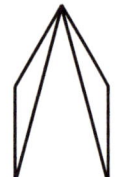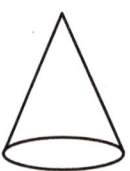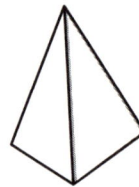

4.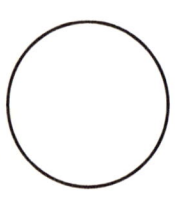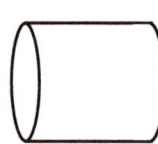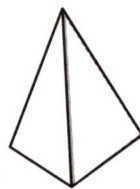

THINK

Name at least one polygon that is not the face for any of the solid figures shown.

Modeling   Name _____   Date _____

Patterns of Solid Figures

Directions: Look at each pattern. Draw the next solid figure in the pattern.

1.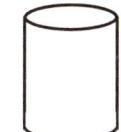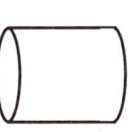

2.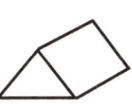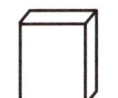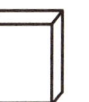

Directions: Create a pattern of solid figures using each set of solid figures.

3.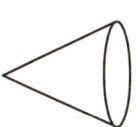

4.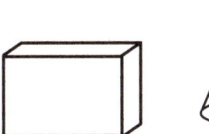

THINK

 Explain your pattern from question 3 or 4. Why is it a pattern?

Modeling Name _____ Date _____

Making a Cube

The **net** of a solid figure is a 2-dimensional drawing of the faces of a 3-dimensional solid figure. When the drawing is folded on its dotted lines, the solid figure is formed.

Directions: Cut out the net below. Fold on the dotted lines shown. Tape the edges to form a cube.

cube

Modeling   Name _____   Date _____

Making a Pyramid

Directions: Cut out the net below. Fold on the dotted lines shown. Tape the edges to form a square pyramid.

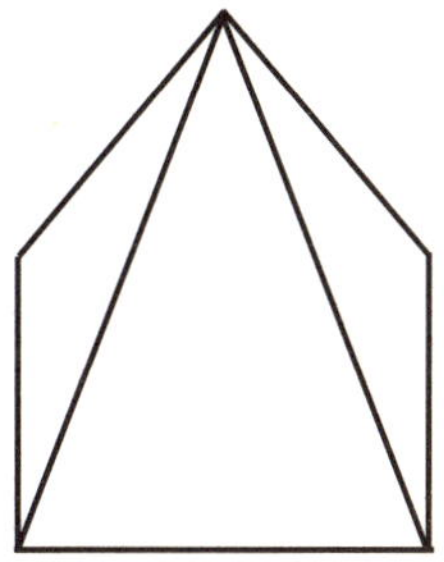

square pyramid

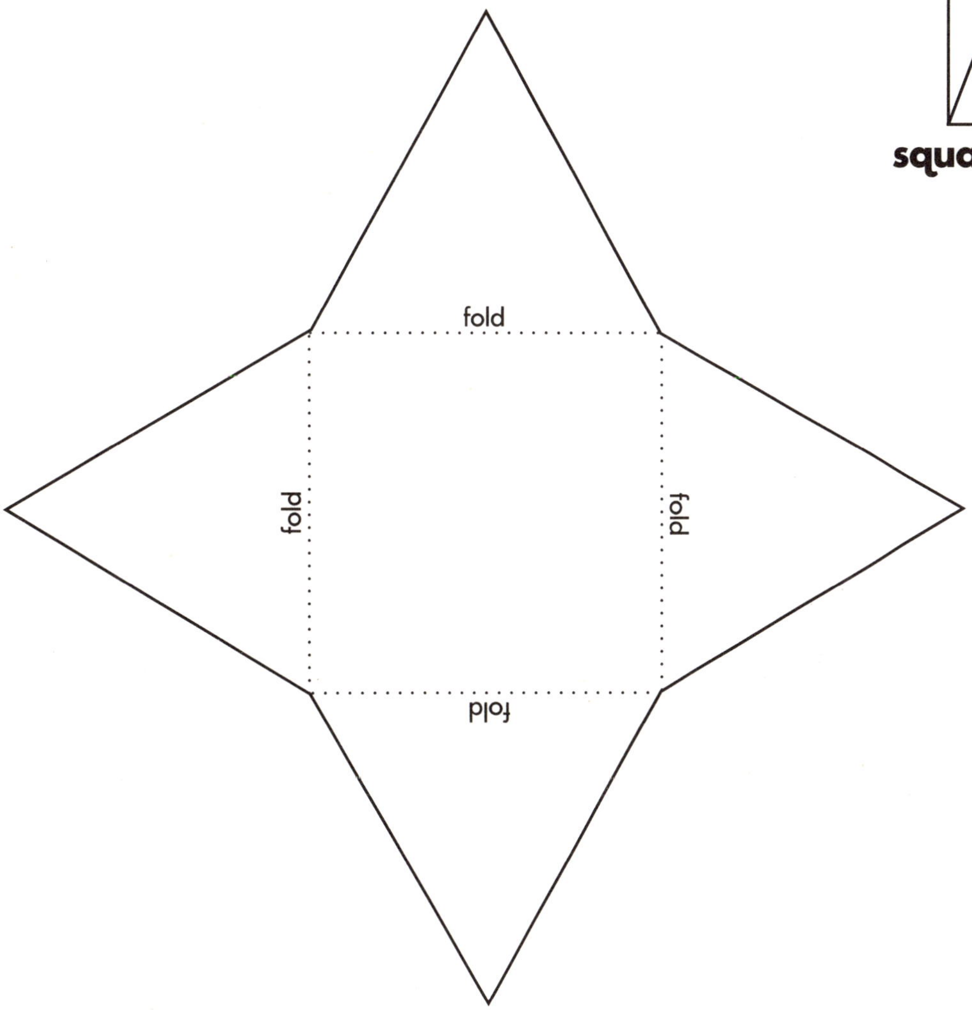

fold

fold

fold

fold

Modeling

Name _____ Date _____

Draw the Nets

Directions: Decide what solid figure each object models.
Sketch a net for the object.
(Ignore the contents inside each solid figure.)

1.

2.

THINK

Neither of these two real-world objects has a top face.
Place an X on each face that should not be included in your nets.

Modeling

Name _____ Date _____

Drawing Shapes

Directions: Follow each direction.

1. Draw a plane figure with 12 sides.

2. Draw a solid figure that can roll.

3. Draw a solid figure that has two circles as its faces.

4. Draw a plane figure that has two pairs of parallel sides.

5. Draw a solid figure with a right angle.

Modeling   Name _____ Date _____

What Will I Make?

Directions: Draw a line to match the description with the correct shape.

1. 6 square faces

2. 1 square, 4 triangles

3. 4 sides, 2 obtuse angles, 2 acute angles

4. 4 sides of equal length

5. 1 right angle, 2 acute angles

6. 8 angles and 8 sides

7. 1 rectangle, 2 circular bases

8. 3 acute angles

9. 2 triangles, 3 rectangles

10. 1 circular base

11. 1 obtuse angle, 2 acute angles

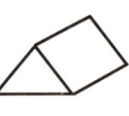

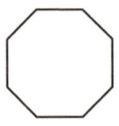
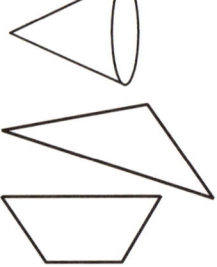
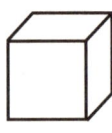

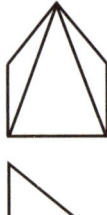

Modeling Name _____ Date _____

Perimeters on Dot Paper

Perimeter is the distance around a figure.

Directions: Find the perimeter of each shape.

1. perimeter of A _____ units
2. perimeter of B _____ units
3. perimeter of C _____ units
4. perimeter of D _____ units

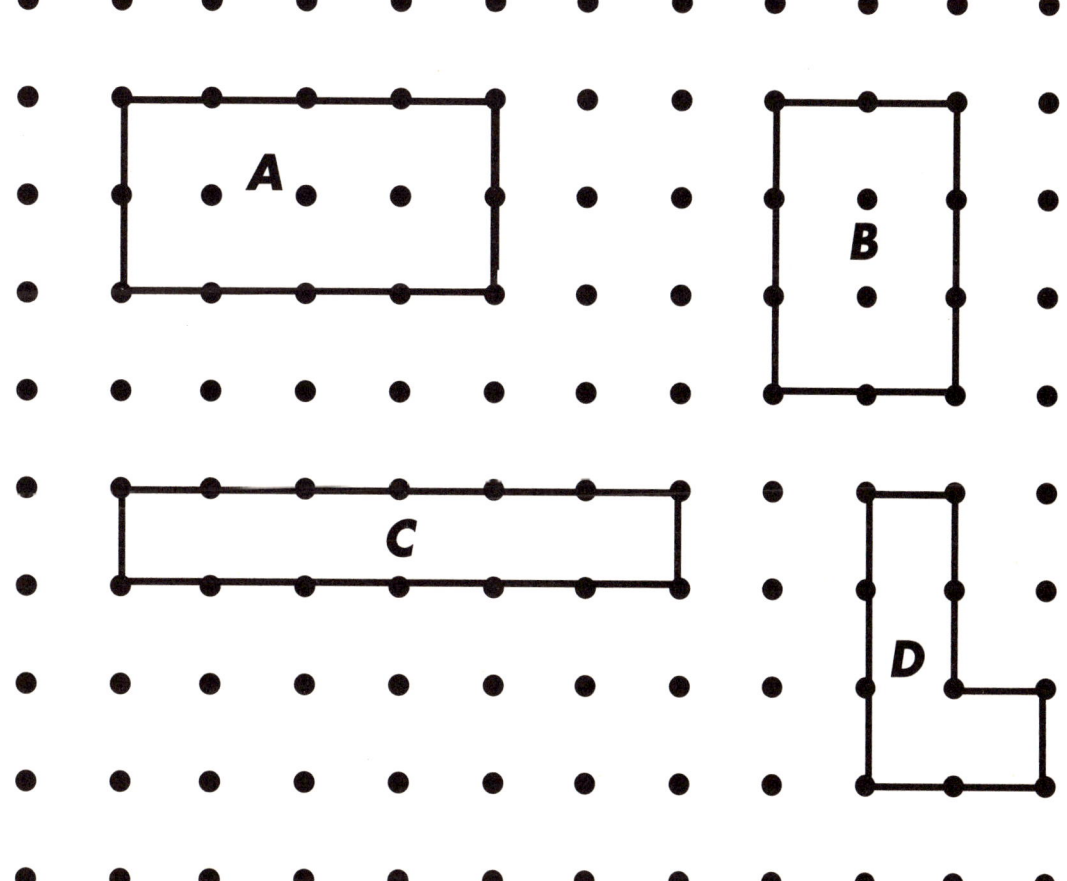

Modeling

Name _____ Date _____

Playground Perimeter

Directions: Solve the problem.

Kevin works at a park that has a new playground. Today is the grand opening. He needs to put a yellow ribbon all the way around the perimeter of the park. How many yards of ribbon does Kevin need?

50 yards

_____ yards

20 yards

30 yards

100 yards

65 yards

100 yards

Areas on Dot Paper

Area is the number of square units in the interior region of a plane figure.

Directions: Find the area of each shape.

1. area of S _____ square units
2. area of T _____ square units
3. area of U _____ square units
4. area of V _____ square units

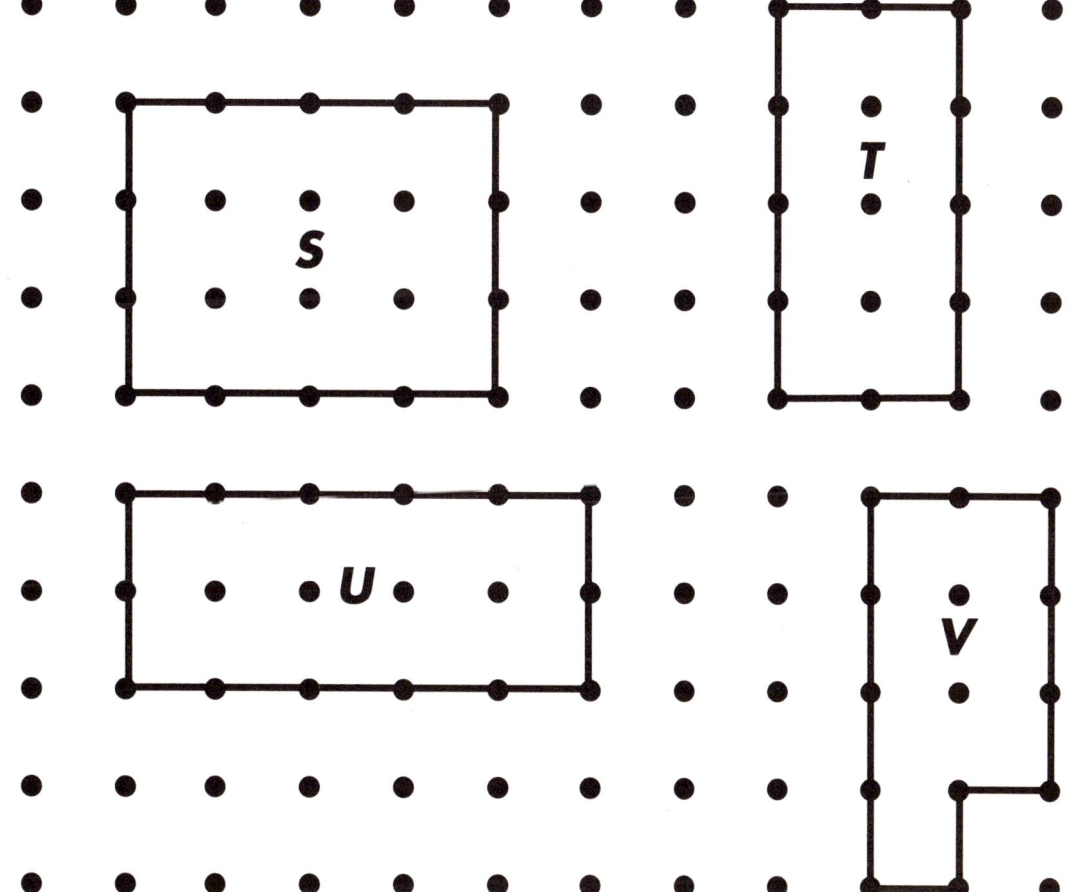

Modeling

Name _____ Date _____

Dollhouse Area

Directions: Solve the problem.

Sally's dad is helping her put carpet on the floors of her dollhouse. Use the floor plan below to find the amount of carpet Sally needs.

_____ square feet

```
family room            bath      
1.5 feet × 2 feet    1.5 feet × 1 feet    bedroom
                                          1 feet × 2 feet
kitchen
1.5 feet × 2 feet
```

"I find the area to know how much carpet to buy."

"I think blue carpet will look best."

102

Modeling Name _____ Date _____

Perimeter or Area

Directions: Read each situation. Decide if the problem is asking about perimeter or area. Circle the appropriate answer choice.

1. Leo is putting up a fence around his garden.
   How much fencing should he buy?   perimeter   area

2. Sara walks around her neighborhood block for exercise.
   How far does she walk?   perimeter   area

3. Hector is painting his bedroom walls.
   How much paint should he buy?   perimeter   area

4. Lou is putting wood trim around his dining room.
   How much wood trim does he need?   perimeter   area

5. Dina is mowing her lawn.
   How many square feet of grass does she cut?   perimeter   area

6. Mrs. Ling is sewing lace around the bedspread.
   How much lace does she sew?   perimeter   area

7. The circus master puts a net under the trapeze acrobats.
   How big is the net?   perimeter   area

DO MORE

Describe a situation about perimeter different than those above.
Describe a situation about area different than those above.

A Different View

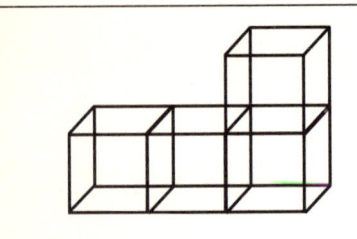

Arrangement of 4 cubes

Below are 2-dimensional views of the group of cubes at the left.

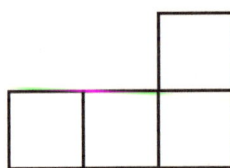

front and back views

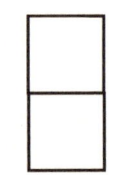

side views

Directions: Sketch the front and back views, and side views of each arrangement.

1.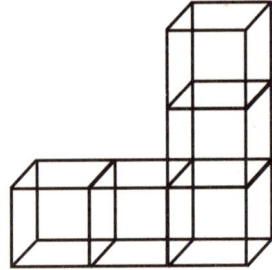

front and back views

side views

2.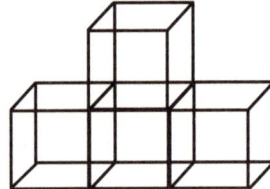

front and back views

side views

Build from a View

Directions: Look at each of the views below. Use cubes to build each 3-dimensional arrangement.

1.

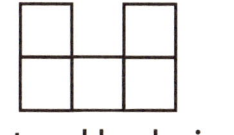

front and back views

side views

2.

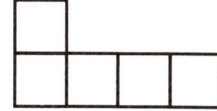

front and back views

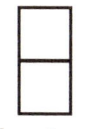

side views

Directions: Use 6 cubes to build a 3-dimensional arrangement. Sketch the front and back views, and the side views.

3.

front and back views   side views

Create Your Own Problems

1. Write a question about drawing shapes on dot paper.

2. Write a word problem that involves drawing a triangle.

3. Write instructions about how to draw a triangular prism.

4. Write a question about a solid figure and its faces.

5. Write a story problem about something in your home that involves perimeter.

Name ______________________ Date ________________

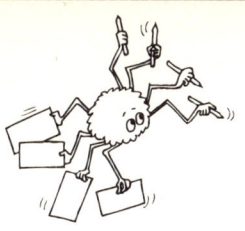

Check Your Skills

1. Which shape is modeled by a stop sign?

____

2. Draw the next three shapes in the pattern.

 ______ ______ ______

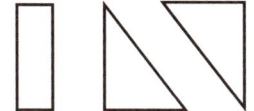

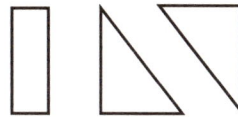

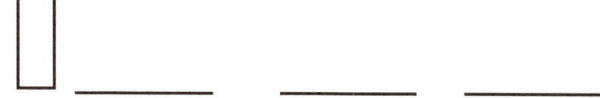

3. Name two solid figures that have at least one circle as a face.

________________ ________________

4. Draw a solid figure that cannot roll.

5. Which shape has 3 acute angles and all of its sides equal in length?

____

0-7424-2983-0 *Using the Standards: Geometry*

Modeling

Check Your Skills (cont.)

6. What is the area of a square with one side 4 centimeters long?

_____

7. What is the perimeter of a regular pentagon with one side 3 centimeters long?

_____

8. Draw a net for a cube.

9. Which plane figure can have one pair of parallel sides, 2 obtuse angles, and 2 acute angles?

_____

10. What is the perimeter of the chalkboard below?

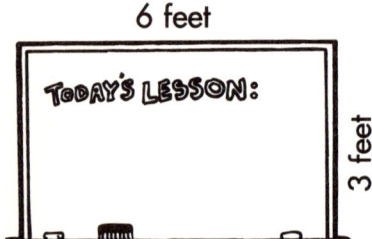

6 feet
3 feet

_____

Name _____ Date _____

Post Test

1. Circle the set of lines that are perpendicular.

   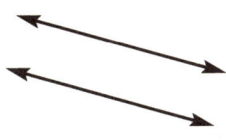   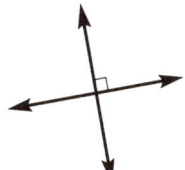

2. What is the name of the plane figure below?

      _____

3. Name a solid figure that has 8 edges and 5 faces?

   _____

4. Name the ordered pairs for each vertex of the shape shown.

   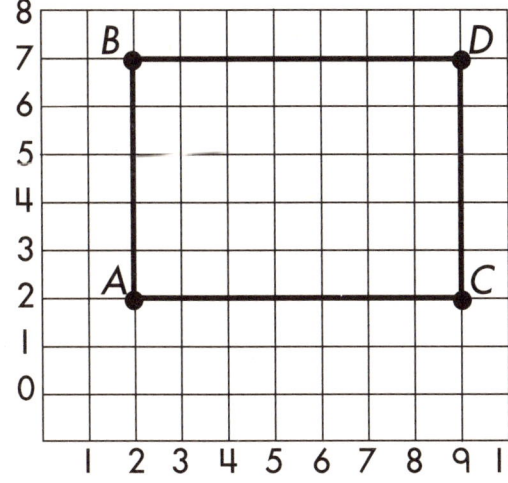

   A _____

   B _____

   C _____

   D _____

5. What is the length of line segment DC shown above? _____

Post Test (cont.)

6. How many lines of symmetry does the plane figure below have?

 _____

7. What transformation is shown?

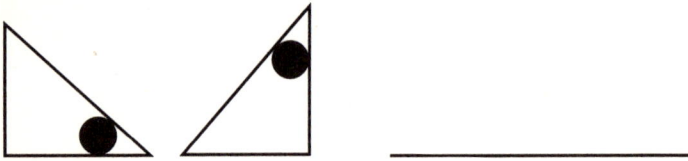 _____

8. Are the shapes below congruent? Write yes or no.

 _____

9. What is the perimeter of a regular octagon with sides 6 centimeters long?

_____

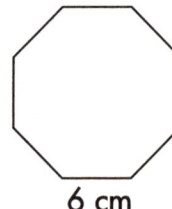

6 cm

10. What is the area of the figure below?

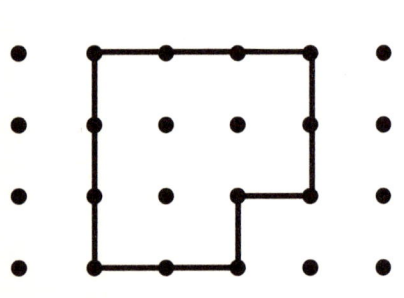

_____

Answer Key

Pretest 7–8
1.  [arrows diagram]
2. yes
3. Figure A
4. A (1, 3), B (3, 7), C (7, 4)
5. 2
6. 4 units
7. slide
8.  [square]

Intersecting and Parallel Lines 9
1. intersecting lines
2. parallel lines
3. parallel lines
4. intersecting lines
5. parallel lines

THINK: Answers will vary but should include looking for the pairs of lines that did not cross each other.

The Size of Angles 10
1. right angle
2. less than a right angle
3. greater than a right angle
4. right angle
5. less than a right angle

Which Angle Is Which? 11
In the top row the first angle has a box around it. The middle and last angles are circled. In the middle row the first angle has a box around it. The middle and last angles are circled. In the bottom row the first and middle angles have boxes around them. The last angle is circled.

THINK: Answers will vary.

What Did the Right Angle Say? 12–13
1. A
2. M
3. U
4. E
5. T

I am used to make a square.

Parallel and Perpendicular Lines 14
1. perpendicular
2. neither
3. neither
4. parallel
5. parallel
6. perpendicular

THINK: parallel lines, perpendicular lines

The Angles of Time 15
1. right angle
2. acute angle
3. acute angle
4. obtuse angle
5. obtuse angle
6. right angle

THINK: 6 o'clock and 12 o'clock

All Circle Round the Polygons 16
All objects except the four shown below are circled.

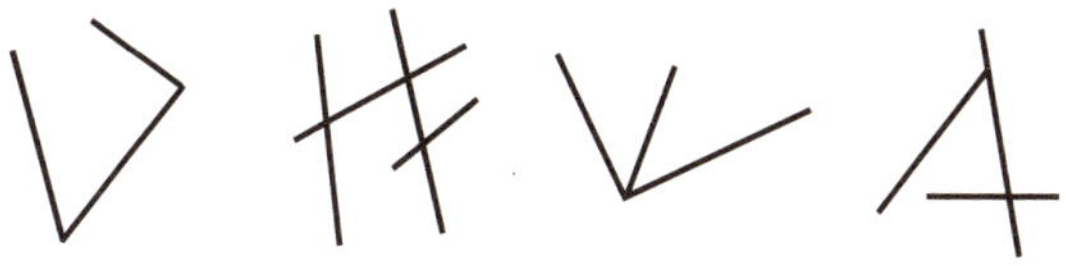

[shapes crossed out]

THINK: Answers will vary.

Shape to Shape 17
1. rectangle
2. octagon
3. triangle
4. circle

DO MORE: Drawings will vary. Samples are shown.

trapezoid   square   parallelogram   hexagon

Plane Figures 18
1. F, H
2. A, C, J, L
3. E, G, I
4. B, D, E, G, K, (If students did not count the squares as rectangles only, their answers will be B, D, K)

Sides and Vertices 19
1. 3, 3
2. 4, 4
3. 4, 4
4. 5, 5
5. 8, 8

Answer Key

More About Sides and Vertices 20
1. Each had the same number of vertices as number of sides.
2. 7
3. 9
4. 8
5. pentagon; Pictures will vary. Sample drawing is shown.
6. hexagon; Pictures will vary. Sample drawing is shown.

DO MORE: Drawings will vary. Samples are shown.

Quadrilateral Names 21
1. quadrilateral, parallelogram
2. quadrilateral, trapezoid
3. quadrilateral, parallelogram, rectangle, square
4. quadrilateral
5. quadrilateral, parallelogram, rectangle

DO MORE: quadrilateral parallelogram, rectangle, rhombus

Divide and Conquer 22
Drawings will vary. Samples are shown.

DO MORE: Drawings will vary.

Drawing Triangles Based on Sides 23
Drawings will vary. Samples are shown.

Drawing Triangles Based on Angles 24
Drawings will vary. Samples are shown.

THINK: one, one

A Race to the Finish 25
Play game. Outcomes will vary.

Which Shape Was Drawn? 26

DO MORE: Answers will vary.

How Many Faces and Edges? 27
1. 6, 12
2. 4, 6
3. 5, 8
4. 6, 12

Plane and Solid Figures 28
1. solid figure
2. plane figure
3. plane figure
4. solid figure

Solid Figures 29
1. sphere
2. rectangular prism
3. cone
4. cylinder
5. sphere
6. cone

Can You Find the Hidden Shapes? 30–31
1. A-balloons, B-baseball, G-basketball
2. A-party hat
3. D-glasses, E-paint cans, F-soda can
4. A-presents, C-seat of the chair, E-table top

Published by Instructional Fair. Copyright protected.

Answer Key

What Solid Figure Am I? 32
Drawings will vary. Sample drawings are shown.
1. cube
2. cone
3. square pyramid
4. sphere
5. rectangular prism

DO MORE: Answers will vary.

Exploring Solid Figures 33
1. C
2. A

Be a Builder 34
Drawings will vary. Samples are shown.
1.
2.
3.
4.

THINK: Answers will vary.

Creating Similar Polygons 35
Drawings are not actual size, but are shown to scale.
1. 0.5 inch, 1 inch
2. 4 inches, 2 inches

THINK: Answers will vary. Possible answer: For the rectangle, I divided each side's length by 2. For the triangle, I multiplied each side's length by 4.

Symmetry in Letters 36
A B C D E H
I M O T U V
W X Y

THINK: H, O, X

Crossword Shapes 37-38
Across
2. sphere
3. circle
5. triangle
7. cube
9. cylinder
10. square

Down
1. vertex
4. rectangle
6. edge
8. pyramid

Create Your Own Problems 39
Answers will vary.

Answer Key

Check Your Skills 40-41
1. Drawings will vary. Sample drawing is shown.
2. It is not a closed figure.
3. 3
4. no; An equilateral triangle has three 60° angles. An obtuse angle is greater than 90°.
5. □
6. 4
7. circle
8. 3
9. cone
10. 12
11. I, O

Going Places 42
1. 4
2. 7
3. 5
4. Police Station

THINK: Answers will vary but should include a note about the compass rose on the map.

Following the Course 43
Sam is at B. Elyse is at E. Jon is at C. Rita is at A.

Reveal the Hidden Message 44-45
Message reads: I ♥ MATH
DO MORE: Answers will vary.

Polygon Point Plotting 46

parallelogram

Name the Vertices 47
1. A (2, 6), B (7, 8), C (6, 2)
2. S (8, 8), T (8, 3), U (2, 1)
3. D (2, 4), E (2, 1), F (7, 1), G (7, 4), H (5, 7)
4. L (2, 7), M (6, 7), N (9, 4), P (5, 4)

THINK: Answers will vary. Possible answer: counted right 5, and up 4

Where Is Mr. Smith Going? 48
Mr. Smith stopped at point (1, 6).

One Point Makes All The Difference 49

Graph A:

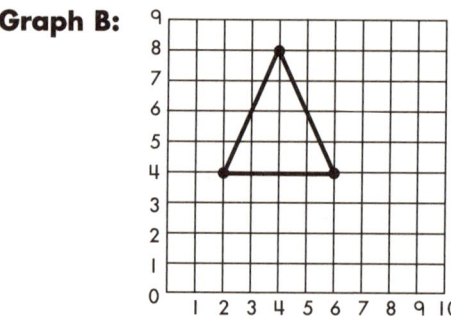

right isosceles triangle

Graph B:

isosceles triangle

Answers will vary but should include that none of the segments are perpendicular now.

Crazy for Coasters 50
1. (9, 14)
2. (15, 1)
3. (5, 9)
4. (3, 4)
5. highest point of the small loop

Answer Key

More About Graphing Points 51

11. Answers can be any of the points F, G, K.
12. Answers can be any point but F, G.
13. Answers can be any point but E, K, J.
14. point H

THINK: Point W can be (9, 6) or (1, 6).

How Far From Point to Point? 52

1. 6 units
2. 3 units
3. 6 units
4. 5 units
5. 3 units
6. 4 units
7. 2 units
8. 5 units

THINK: Answers will vary.

Locate the Endpoints 53

1. (8, 4)
2. (0, 5)
3. (7, 2)
4. (6, 4)
5. (5, 2.5) or (5, 7.5)

THINK: The first coordinate number is always the same. The second coordinate number is always the same.

From Here to There 54

1. B2
2. B2
3. B1
4. C2
5. Answers will vary. Possible answer: right 2, and up 1
6. Answers will vary. Possible answer: left 1, and down 1

Who Gets There First? 55

1. Hector
2. Abbey
3. They walk the same distance.

THINK: a right angle

Making a Course 56

Grids and directions will vary.

Carving a Jack-o-Lantern 57

Designs and ordered pairs will vary.

Drawing Lines of Symmetry 58

DO MORE: Drawings will vary.

Create with Symmetry 59

1. (6, 8.5)
2. (7, 9)
3. (8, 9)
4. (8.5, 8.5)
5. (9, 7)
6. (8.5, 5)
7. (7.5, 4)
8. (6, 3)

Reflect Each Other 60

Grids and points will vary.

Answer Key

Look in the Mirror 61

1.

2.

3.

4.

THINK: Answers will vary.

Create Your Own Problems 62

Answers will vary.

Check Your Skills 63–64

1. (8, 7)
2.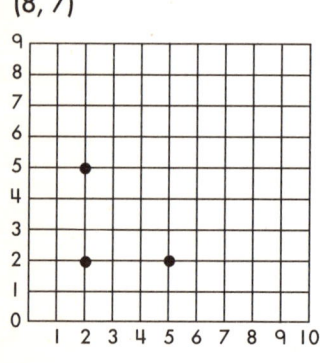

   (5, 5)

3.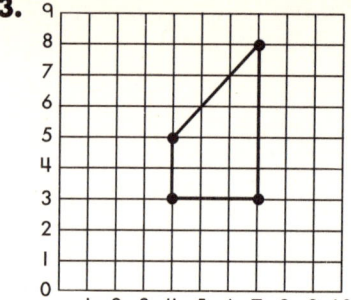

   trapezoid
4. A
5. F
6. 5 units
7. Answers will vary. Sample answer: slide right 3 units, down 1 unit.

Flips, Slides, and Turns 65

1.
2.
3.
4.
5.

Match the Transformation 66

1.
2.
3.
4.
5.

Answer Key

Are You Seeing Double? 67
1. no
2. yes, flip
3. no
4. no
5. yes, turn
6. yes, slide

Slide from Start to Finish 68

Transforming Letters 69
1. Ǝ W W E E
2. V < > > V
3. ⊳ A A A A
4. И N N Z N

THINK: V and A

Transforming a Clown 70

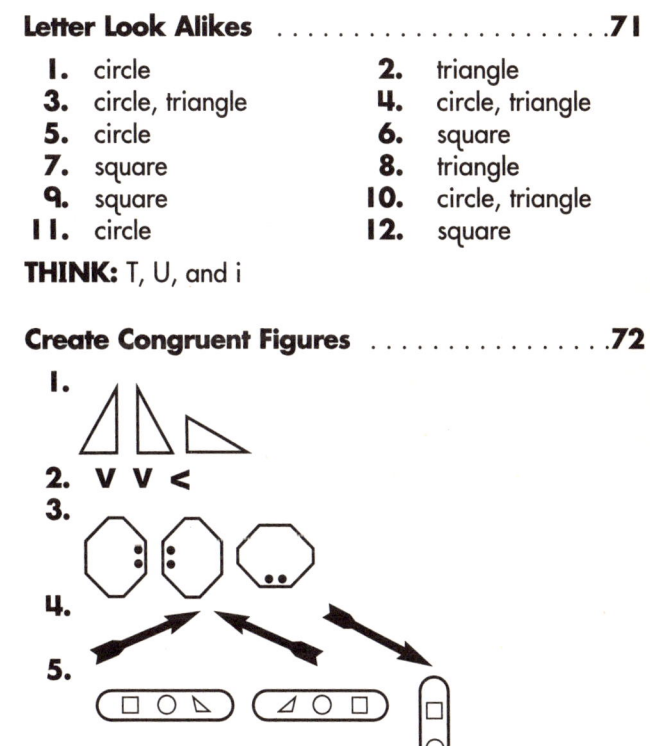

slide

Letter Look Alikes .71
1. circle
2. triangle
3. circle, triangle
4. circle, triangle
5. circle
6. square
7. square
8. triangle
9. square
10. circle, triangle
11. circle
12. square

THINK: T, U, and i

Create Congruent Figures 72

Moving to the Next Location 73
1. slide
2. vertical flip
3. horizontal flip
4. slide
5. slide
6. turn
7. turn
8. slide
9. vertical flip
10. turn

Answer Key

Lines of Symmetry 74
1. no 2. yes 3. no
4. yes 5. no 6. no

THINK: Answers will vary.

Many Lines of Symmetry 75
1. 4 2. 3 3. 1 4. 0
5. 4 6. 2 7. 0

Point Symmetry 76
1. yes 2. yes 3. yes
4. yes 5. no 6. no

Pictures with Point Symmetry 77
1.
2.

Arrange Flowers 78

Drawings will vary.

DO MORE: Answers will vary.

Create Your Own Problems 79

Answers will vary.

Check Your Skills 80–81
1. Answers will vary. Possible answers include A, V, and U.
2. 5
3. flip
4. flip
5.
6.
7.

8. yes
9. a. vertical flip
   b. horizontal flip

Shape Scavenger Hunt 82

Answers will vary.

THINK: Answers will vary.

Patterns of Shapes 83
1.   2.
3.   4.

THINK: 3; 1, 2, and 4

Use Dot Paper to Draw 84

Drawings will vary. Samples are shown.

THINK: Answers will vary but should include something about knowing the lengths of the line segments.

Isosceles Drawings 85

Drawings will vary. Samples are shown.

Answer Key

THINK: Answers will vary but should include that the dots can be used to create lines of the same length.

Triangle Types 86
Drawings will vary. Samples are shown.

1. 2.
3. 4.
5. 6.

Draw Quadrilaterals 87
Drawings will vary. Samples are shown.

1.
2.
3.
4.
5.
6.

THINK: trapezoid and isosceles trapezoid

Solid Figure Scavenger Hunt 88
Answers will vary.
THINK: Answers will vary.

Rectangular Prism Dot-to-Dot 89

DO MORE:

Square Pyramid Dot-to-Dot 90

DO MORE:

Face by Face 91
1. 4, 2
2. 1, 4
3. 1, 1
4. 6
5. 2, 1

The Face That Does Not Belong 92
1.
2.
3.
4.

THINK: Answers will vary. Sample answer: trapezoid

Patterns of Solid Figures 93
1. 2.

Patterns will vary for 3 and 4.
THINK: Answers will vary.

Making a Cube 94
Cut out, fold, and make cube.

Answer Key

Making a Pyramid 95
Cut out, fold, and make pyramid.

Draw the Nets 96
1. cylinder
2. rectangular prism

THINK: The nets above show the x on the faces that should not be included.

Drawing Shapes 97
Drawings will vary. Samples are shown.
1. 2. 3.
4. 5.

What Will I Make? 98
1. 2. 3.
4. 5. 6.
7. 8. 9.
10. 11.

Perimeters on Dot Paper 99
1. 12 2. 10 3. 14 4. 10

Playground Perimeter 100
365

Areas on Dot Paper 101
1. 12 2. 8 3. 10 4. 7

Dollhouse Area 102
9.5

Perimeter or Area 103
1. perimeter   2. perimeter   3. area
4. perimeter   5. area   6. perimeter
7. area

DO MORE: Answers will vary.

A Different View 104
1. 2.

Build from a View 105
Use cubes to build arrangements.

Create Your Own Problems 106
Answers will vary.

Check Your Skills 107–108
1. octagon
2.
3. cone, cylinder
4. Drawings will vary. Sample is shown.
5. equilateral triangle
6. 16 square centimeters
7. 15 centimeters
8.
9. trapezoid
10. 18 feet

Post Test 109–110
1.
2. trapezoid
3. rectangular pyramid
4. A(2, 2), B(2, 7), C(9, 2), D(9, 7)
5. 5 units   6. 0
7. turn   8. no
9. 48 centimeters 10. 8 square units

acute angle	edge
equilateral triangle	face
flip	intersecting lines

a line segment where two faces of a solid figure meet	an angle that has a measure less than 90°
a flat surface of a solid figure	a triangle with 3 sides of equal length
lines that cross each other at one point	a transformation that creates a mirror image of the original image

isosceles triangle	line of symmetry
obtuse angle	ordered pair
parallel lines	parallelogram

a line that divides a picture or shape into two halves that are mirror images of each other	a triangle with 2 sides of equal length
a pair of numbers that describes the location of a point on a coordinate grid	an angle that has a measure greater than 90°
a quadrilateral with 2 pairs of parallel sides	lines that do not intersect each other

perpendicular lines	polygon
quadrilateral	rectangle
right angle	scalene triangle

a closed plane figure that is formed by 3 or more line segments	lines that intersect to form right angles
a parallelogram with 4 right angles	a four-sided plane figure
a triangle that has no sides of equal length	an angle that has a measure of 90°

slide	square
trapezoid	triangle
turn	vertex

a rectangle with 4 sides of equal length	a transformation that creates an image moved from the location of the original image
a three-sided plane figure	a quadrilateral with only one pair of parallel sides
a point where two line segments meet	a transformation that creates a rotated image of the original image